Everyday
Church

Everyday Church

mission by being good neighbours

Tim Chester & Steve Timmis

ivp

INTER-VARSITY PRESS
Norton Street, Nottingham NG7 3HR, England
Email: ivp@ivpbooks.com
Website: www.ivpbooks.com

First published 2011

British Library Cataloguing in Publication Data
A catalogue record for this book is available from the British Library.

ISBN: 978–1–84474–520–3

Set in 12/15pt Garamond
Typeset in Great Britain by Servis Filmsetting Ltd, Stockport, Cheshire
Printed and bound in Great Britain by Ashford Colour Press Ltd, Gosport, Hampshire

CONTENTS

INTRODUCTION

In 1915 Tim's grandmother moved to a two-up, two-down terraced house in Darlington, an industrial town in the north of England. She was one year old. The street was still being built when she moved there. So too was the Methodist chapel two streets away. That house became her home for the next ninety years, and the chapel became a second home.

When my mother was a child, the congregation was 100 strong, with a choir of twenty, plus another fifty children in the Sunday school. More than that, the church was at the heart of neighbourhood life. Church concerts, church teas, church outings – these were the only working-class alternatives to the pub. My grandmother and my mother grew up with the church at the very centre of their lives.

My grandmother was still playing the piano on a Sunday

morning in her nineties. Her increasing deafness meant she had trouble hearing the singing, but there was no-one else to take over. The congregation has now dwindled to just a dozen or so, none of whom are under fifty. Local people have other things to do on a Sunday morning. Choir recitals cannot compete with the Xbox and *The X Factor*. The building, freshly built when my grandmother started attending, has become a relic, a monument to a former way of life. It plays no part in the lives of all but a handful of people. It is part of the neighbourhood's history, but not of its present.

Christians today increasingly find ourselves on the margins of our culture. In fact, we live in a post-Christian culture. The majority of people in the West have no intention of ever attending church. Most only utter the name of Christ as a swear word. Some prominent churches are growing, but much of this is transfer growth rather than true evangelistic growth.

Yet many of our approaches to evangelism still assume a Christendom mentality. We expect people to come when we ring the church bell or put on a good service. But the majority of the population are disconnected. Changing what we do in church will not reach them. We need to meet them in the context of everyday life.

Our previous book, *Total Church*,[1] argued that the Christian gospel and the Christian community should be central to every aspect of our life and mission. This book builds upon that foundation. It is a call for us to be *an everyday church with an everyday mission*. We need to shift our focus from putting on attractional events to creating attractional communities. Our marginal status is an opportunity to rediscover the missionary call of the people of God. We can recover witness to Christ, unmuddied by nominal Christianity.

Our marginal status is also an opportunity to reconnect

with our Bibles. The New Testament is a collection of missionary documents written to missionary situations. It was written by Christians living on the margins of their culture. Throughout this book, we will enter into a dialogue with the first letter of Peter. Peter was writing to Christians who found themselves 'strangers and exiles' in the first-century Roman Empire. They were on the margins facing slander and abuse much as we are. This book is not a commentary. Instead, we want to offer some missional reflections on 1 Peter, to explore what the Holy Spirit would say to the Western church today through this portion of God's Word. Above all, we have tried to write a practical book that shows what everyday church and everyday mission might look like on the ground.

In calling the church to everyday mission, we recognize that this is what many, many Christians are already doing: being good neighbours, colleagues, family members, doing good in the face of hostility, bearing witness to Christ in the context of ordinary life. Our aim is not to dismiss this. Quite the opposite. We want to celebrate it and put it back at the centre of the church's mission. And perhaps also give it more direction and show how it can be more intentional.

One final note. We have written this book together and so generally use plural pronouns (we, us). But where we describe an experience or story particular to one of us, we have used a singular pronoun (I, me).

1. LIFE AT THE MARGINS

1 Peter 1:1–12

It's easy for us Christians to feel discouraged when we read about declining church attendance or see the growing secularization of our culture. But we are excited about the future. In many ways the opposite of secularism was actually nominalism. So growing secularism is an opportunity to develop witness to Christ, unclouded by nominal faith. Much of the decline in the church in the West has been the falling off of nominal Christians. As a result, what remains may be more healthy. We now have the opportunity to become communities focused on Jesus and his mission. The number of true Christians may not be falling so steeply – if at all. But what is fast disappearing is the opportunity to reach notionally religious people through church activities.

To seize these opportunities we first need to recognize

that the Christian gospel has moved from the centre of our culture to the margins.

Living in a post-Christian context

When we (the Chesters) first moved into our home, we got talking with our new neighbour, an elderly woman who lives alone. During the conversation, we told her we had moved to the area to be part of a new church. 'I'm glad you're Christians,' she told us, before adding that she too was a Christian. It turns out, however, that she never attends church and she has since resisted all our attempts to talk to her about Jesus. So what did she mean when she said she was a Christian? Perhaps she meant that she was a nice person and good neighbour (which she is). Perhaps she meant she was not a Muslim – her neighbours on the other side are a Muslim family originating from Pakistan, as are perhaps a third of the people living on our road. What is clear is that she did not mean she is a Christian by any biblical definition of the word. To her, 'Christian' is a cultural or ethnic label. It is not a declaration of her faith in Jesus as her Saviour, nor her allegiance to him as her Lord, nor her membership of his redeemed people.

I think of my neighbour when I hear that, according to the 2001 UK Government Census, 72% of the UK population claim to be Christian. From this we might suppose that the UK is a Christian country, with little need for church planting. But figures for church attendance reveal a very different picture. In 1851, around 1 in 4 people in the UK were churchgoers. Now it is 1 in 10,[1] though only about half of these are actually in church on any given Sunday.[2] Of these, 40% go to evangelical churches.[3] If present trends continue, average weekly church attendance in England will fall to 4.1% in 2020.[4] That's 1 in 25.

Philip Richter and Leslie Francis categorize people as 'churched' (regular or fringe churchgoers), 'de-churched' (people who have been regular or fringe churchgoers at some point in the past, but are so no longer) and 'non-churched' or 'un-churched' (people who have had no significant contact with the church at any point).[5] Based on their findings, the *Mission-Shaped Church* report concluded that the UK population is 20% churched, 40% de-churched and 40% non-churched.[6] A 2007 Tearfund report found that almost 70% of the UK population have no intention of attending a church service at any point in the future.[7] And this figure is set to increase over the coming years with affiliation to Christianity and attendance at church lower among young people. Only a third of sixteen-to-thirty-four-year-olds even call themselves Christians.

Seventy per cent of the UK population have no intention of ever attending a church service. That means new styles of worship will not reach them. Fresh expressions of church will not reach them. Alpha and Christianity Explored courses will not reach them. Guest services will not reach them. Churches meeting in pubs will not reach them. Toddler churches meeting at the end of the school day will not reach them. The vast majority of un-churched and de-churched people would not turn to the church, even if faced with difficult personal circumstances or in the event of national tragedies.[8] It is not a question of 'improving the product' of church meetings and evangelistic events. It means reaching people *apart from* meetings and events.

Despite the fall in overall church attendance, only 1 in 6 regular churchgoers thinks the church they attend is declining in numbers. Two-fifths actually think their church is growing.[9] Perhaps some people are in denial about falling church numbers. But it may also be that many churches are growing, but mainly, as we saw in the Introduction, through transfer growth. A declining number of Christians are 'consolidating' into growing churches. It is still possible to grow a church by offering a better church experience than other churches. Whatever the merits of this, it is vital for us to realize that this is not evangelistic growth. It is possible to plant a church and see it grow *without doing mission*. 'People can be attracted to a church by what it offers,' says Jim Petersen, 'but . . . increase of this sort isn't church growth at all. It's just a reshuffling of the same fifty-two cards.'[10]

In the rest of Europe, church attendance is higher than in the UK in Catholic and Orthodox countries, but all across Europe Christian faith is at best nominal. The ten mega-peoples least responsive to the gospel are all found in Europe, according to the World Christian Database.[11] A report by Greater Europe Mission concludes: 'Although Europe has a high percentage of people who consider themselves Christians, the data show that Europe has the least population percentage of Christians who consider themselves committed and evangelical.'[12] Europe is now the world's most secular continent.

In Australia 68% of people may claim to be Christian, but like the UK this is largely nominal. Church attendance was 8% in 2001, down from 35% in 1966.[13] As in the UK, it is the younger generation who are missing from the Australian church.[14] A church planter in Perth wrote recently: 'Many of my work colleagues are very suspicious of, or hostile to, Christianity . . . I think in my work context in Perth it must be "easier" to be openly and proudly gay than openly and proudly Christian.'[15]

The picture in the United States remains very different. America has a far more Christianized culture than Europe. Research by the Barna Group in 2008 found that only 1 in 4 adults in the United States had no contact with the church, while 62% had attended church in the past month, and a further 15% had had some contact over the past year.[16]

An American friend who has worked in Europe for the last seven years revisited the US recently. Sitting drinking coffee in a McDonald's in Florida, he was shocked to overhear so many people talking about Jesus or church as they queued to order. This doesn't happen in Europe! While 1 in 4 Americans has no contact with church, in Britain it is 3 in 4.[17] Even in the supposedly more secular areas of the North-West and North-East, the un-churched are still a minority.[18] Moreover, among un-churched Americans there is a high level of sympathy for Christianity, and there are even confessions of faith in Christ. Among those not attending church 59% consider themselves to be Christian and 17% express a commitment to Christ and believe they will experience heaven after death through their acceptance of Christ as their Saviour. Furthermore, 19% of those not attending church read the Bible during a typical week and 62% pray.[19]

Yet despite this, 100 million people in the United States have no contact with church.[20] Among this group are an estimated 13–15 million people who express a commitment to Christ and accept him as their Saviour. This still leaves *85 million Americans who are un-churched and unbelieving.*

Two observations are pertinent. First, we cannot assume that models of church growth from the United States will work in Europe. Of course there is much that we can learn from the practice and theology of the American church. Our own experience in The Crowded House is testimony to that. But we cannot automatically import church growth and church planting models. In the United States you can still plant a church by creating a better church experience. If you do this in the UK, then the best you can do is attract existing churchgoers. That might be a valid endeavour, but *it is not evangelistic growth.*

Secondly, parts of the United States are heading in the direction of Europe. It may be time for the US church to learn from the European church's experience of being on the margins of the culture. The Easter 2009 edition of *Newsweek* magazine created a stir with the words 'The decline and fall of Christian America' emblazoned across its front cover. The cover article by Jon Meacham quotes Al Mohler as saying, 'Clearly, there is a new narrative, a post-Christian narrative, that is animating large portions of this society.' The number of adults in the United States who do not attend church has nearly doubled since 1991. Over 3,500 US churches close their doors every year, and the attendance of more than 80% of those remaining has plateaued or is declining.[21] Researcher Mike Regele concludes:

> The combined impact of the Information Age, postmodern thought, globalization, and racial-ethnic pluralism that has seen the demise of the grand American story also has displaced the historic role the church has played in that story. As a result, we are seeing the marginalization of the institutional church.[22]

Since the Enlightenment, Western intellectuals have assumed a link between modernity and secularization. Some rejoiced in this 'progress' while others lamented the reduction of everything to 'rationality', but they shared the assumption that modern societies would become secular societies. However, this 'secularization theory' has been challenged by sociologist Peter Berger. 'Not to put too fine a point on it,' he says, 'they were mistaken. Modernity is *not* intrinsically secularizing, though it has been so in particular cases.'[23] The modern world is not becoming more secular. If anything it is becoming more religious.

But Berger identifies two exceptions. The first is geographic: Western and Central Europe. The second is sociological: the élites of the Western world. Pointing to a survey which named India as the world's most religious country and Sweden as the world's most secular country, Berger quips that the United States is a nation of Indians ruled over by Swedes. In other words, it is a highly religious nation, but its élites are deeply secular, even anti-religious. So America *feels* more secular than it actually is. This has been the experience of Americans coming to do mission in the UK. They thought of the US as a secular context until they came to Europe and encountered secular attitudes not only in the media, but among most ordinary people.

Although he refutes secularization theory, Berger does believe that modernity changes the position of the church in the culture:

> Modernity is not necessarily secularizing; it is necessarily *pluralizing*. Modernity is characterized by an increasing plurality, within the same society, of different beliefs, values, and worldviews. Plurality does indeed pose a challenge to all religious traditions – each one must cope with the fact that there are 'all these others,' not just in a faraway country but right next door.[24]

Pluralism means that, while mainstream America is not secular, this does not necessarily indicate it is Christian. We should not mistake religiosity for biblical faith. In eighteenth-century America, Christianity was the dominant worldview. Not any more. Now Western societies are a melting pot of worldviews. We can no longer assume that if people want to find God or discover meaning or cope with a personal crisis they will go to church. They may attend any number of religious bodies or sects. Or they may go to a therapist. Or read a self-help book. Merely opening our doors each Sunday is no longer sufficient. Offering a good product is not enough.

It may be that Middle America follows the lead of its cities and becomes more secular. Or it may be that America becomes an increasingly divided nation with secular élites, but a religious heartland. What is clear is that great swathes of America will not be reached through Sunday morning services.

George G. Hunter concludes: 'As measured by the simple indicator of church attendance, nations that were once substantially Christian are now largely lost to the Christian movement.'[25]

Living in a post-Christendom context

We are not only living in a post-Christian context but in a post-Christendom context. Christendom is the formal or informal alliance of church and state that was the dominant model in Europe from the conversion of Constantine in the fourth century AD onwards. The state authorized the church while the church supported the state. Christianity became a civil religion. To be born into the states of Europe was to be born into the church. The church as an institution was given special privileges. This mutual legitimization was symbolized in the overtly Christian coronation oaths, parliamentary prayers and sermons, the parish system, the coronation of monarchs by archbishops and so on. The United States formally separated church and state, and allowed for religious toleration. But in other ways Christendom has been as strong in the United States as in Europe. The assumption is that Christianity should have a privileged status in the cultural and political discourse of the nation. Presidents and would-be presidents overtly reference their faith and close their speeches with the words, 'God bless America.'

Christendom, however, is increasingly a spent force in the West. Some of the symbolism remains. The British monarch is still the head of an established church, and bishops still sit in the upper chamber of the UK Parliament. But the reality of Christendom is fading fast, overtaken by secularism and pluralism. The Bible no longer has authority in public discourse. The church no longer has a privileged voice. Church leaders still get invited to state occasions, but on matters of ethics they are ignored. When the Pope visited the UK in 2010 he was greeted with all due pomp and ceremony as a head of state. But when it comes to his views on abortion and homosexuality he is ignored by politicians and ridiculed by the media. Lyndon Bowring, Executive Chairman of CARE, said in a recent interview, 'The greatest challenge . . . is the growing secularization of society, where Christianity is being increasingly squeezed out of our national life. The ultimate result of this tendency will be a society that is hostile to Christian truth and practice.'[26]

In his book *After Christendom* Stuart Murray defines 'post-Christendom' as 'the culture that emerges as the Christian faith loses coherence within a society that has been definitively shaped by the Christian story and as the institutions that have been developed to express Christian convictions decline in influence'. He also identifies seven transitions that mark the shift from Christendom to a post-Christendom culture:

- *From the centre to margins*
  In Christendom the Christian story and the churches were central, but in post-Christendom these are marginal.
- *From majority to minority*
  In Christendom Christians comprised the (often overwhelming) majority, but in post-Christendom we are a minority.

- *From settlers to sojourners*
  In Christendom Christians felt at home in a culture
  shaped by their story, but in post-Christendom we are
  aliens, exiles and pilgrims in a culture where we no
  longer feel at home.
- *From privilege to plurality*
  In Christendom Christians enjoyed many privileges,
  but in post-Christendom we are one community among
  many in a plural society.
- *From control to witness*
  In Christendom churches could exert control
  over society, but in post-Christendom we exercise
  influence only through witnessing to our story and its
  implications.
- *From maintenance to mission*
  In Christendom the emphasis was on maintaining a
  supposedly Christian status quo, but in post-Christendom
  it is on mission within a contested environment.
- *From institution to movement*
  In Christendom churches operated mainly in
  institutional mode, but in post-Christendom we must
  become again a Christian movement.[27]

The legacy of Christendom is hotly debated. Some Christians
recognize that it has come to an end, but believe it leaves a
largely positive legacy. Others celebrate its passing, bemoaning the compromises it imposed on the church. The church's
privileged status in society, they believe, meant it had a vested
interest in the status quo which inevitably blunted its proclamation of the social dimensions of repentance, meaning that
the church was aligned, or was perceived to be aligned, with
the establishment.

The future of Christendom is also debated. Historian

Philip Jenkins predicts a growing non-Western Christendom doing battle with militant Islam across the so-called Third World.[28] Our focus, however, is on the West.

Here some Christians want to hang on to the last vestiges of Christendom, campaigning to retain symbols such as an overtly Christian coronation oath. Or they talk up the statistics of Christian affiliation, however notional. Lynda Barley, Head of Research and Statistics for the Church of England, claims, for example, that 'Britain is still a predominantly Christian country' because when asked in the census about their religion more than seven in ten people consider themselves to be Christian.[29] Yet a 2007 poll found that only 22% of men and 26% of women in Britain agreed with the statement: 'I believe in a personal god who created the world and hears my prayers.'[30] So by any definition of Christian faith almost two-thirds of those who say they are Christians clearly are not, for they do not even believe in a personal God.[31] So why claim that Britain is still a predominantly Christian country? Because some Christians want to retain the notion that our nation is a Christian country with the privileges and securities this brings. It allows us to continue on the basis of 'business as usual'.

The *Mission-Shaped Church* report is more realistic:

> The Christian story is no longer at the heart of the nation. Although people may identify themselves as 'Christian' in the national census, for the majority that does not involve belonging to a worshipping community, or any inclination that it should. Many people have no identifiable religious interest or expression.[32]

But we are not pessimistic. There are many signs of life. Many churches are healthy. We sense a growing commitment to church planting across all the different tribes of evangelicalism. God's Word is still being proclaimed. The gospel is still the power of God for salvation. The Lord's arm is not too short that it cannot save. The Holy Spirit is alive and well. Christ will build his church. Our aim in reviewing these statistics is not to make us give up, but to show that the ways we do mission have to change.

Christendom evangelism in a post-Christendom culture

I, Steve, got into church planting in a strange way. In order to marry the 'woman of my dreams', I sat in the front room of her parents' house, asking her father for her hand in marriage. Her mother intervened: I could marry their daughter if I had a job and a house. It was Easter and I was graduating in June with prospects of neither job nor house. Their daughter, waiting anxiously outside the room, was horrified to hear this stipulation. My girlfriend was even more horrified when she heard me agree. I left the house and cycled 5 miles in the dark to a man in a small village who I knew had an empty building and a desire to start a church. I was twenty-two years old, but in two weeks I had a position and with it the house and job (supplemented by milking cows). We were able to get married within a few months.

On my first day in the job I started knocking on doors in the village. Every door was opened and then closed again. The same happened on the second day. And the third. So on the fourth day I got myself a clerical dog collar. From then on the doors were opened and I was warmly received. Being seen as a member of the clergy still had currency. Respect was still shown to the church. That was thirty years ago. Those days are now long gone.

There is nothing particularly new in our analysis of the demise of Christendom. But most of the attention in the discussion on the future of Christendom has focused on the impact of its demise on the church's involvement in the wider culture and in politics. Few have addressed what it means for the local church.

For all its vital rediscovery of gospel-centred theology the Reformation in Europe did not lead to a recovery of gospel-centred mission by local churches. That was because the Reformers generally accepted the Christendom presupposition that Europe was Christian. To be born was to be born into the church. So the church's mission to the surrounding society was pastoral rather than evangelistic. Later, with the rise of the evangelical movement, evangelism returned 'as a response to the rather belated recognition that Europe was, at best, only nominally Christian'.

> But evangelism was still operating within a Christendom framework.
> Within Europe, it was assumed that the Christian story and the main
> tenets of the Christian message were familiar, so evangelism primarily
> involved repeated attempts to re-energize faith and commitment
> that seemed lukewarm. The emphasis was on calling people to make
> a renewed commitment to the implications of the gospel and to
> express this by activities such as reading the Bible, attending church
> more regularly, living morally respectable lives, and meeting the
> needs of others in a society without a welfare state. Beyond Europe,
> despite the heroic and often exemplary efforts of dedicated pioneer
> missionaries, evangelism too often degenerated into attempts to
> coerce or induce conversion and to impose a supposedly Christian
> and superior European culture on other societies.[33]

As a student Tim belonged to a lively, evangelistic church. Each Sunday evening someone was interviewed at the front and asked how they had become a Christian. Week after week the same phrase kept cropping up: 'My faith came alive.' Most stories were of people who attended church as a child, but only now had their 'faith come alive'. Evangelistic fruit came from, as Murray puts it, 'attempts to re-energize faith'. And fruit there truly was. Nominal Christians were becoming living Christians. It was a joy to hear those stories each week. But the opportunities to 're-energize faith' are diminishing fast as our culture becomes post-Christian.

However, most of our current dominant models of church and evangelism are Christendom models. And this needs to change as we move to a post-Christendom and post-Christian context.

Because we regard people as innately Christian in orientation, we think we can reach them through church meetings. So we invite them to our Sunday services or traditional celebrations in the church calendar (such as Christmas, Easter and harvest) or special guest services or evangelistic courses (such as Alpha or Christianity Explored). At The Crowded House we've often been asked how we do mission without a noticeboard or public front door. 'What about people who want to wander in off the streets?' people ask. The assumption is that mission equals a public presence. We ring the church bell and expect people to come to our meetings to hear the gospel.

We also build evangelism around the traditional rites of passage, connecting through christenings, marriages and funerals. We use baptism and marriage classes to present the gospel. We use these occasions to invite people to attend church regularly. Or, to put it more colloquially, we reach people through the opportunities presented by 'hatch, match and dispatch'.

A Christendom model seeks to exploit our perceived privileged status on the high street. We assume that a dog collar will still open doors and that members of the clergy will have a position of standing in society. We assume that events advertised on our noticeboard will draw people into the building and that we ought to be able to conduct assemblies in local schools. We assume that we have a right to be heard when this is no longer the case, and this means we are perceived as strident and self-interested.

There is nothing wrong with any of these endeavours. In fact there's a lot that is right with them. But they are fading opportunities. The number of christenings, church weddings and church funerals is falling, as is attendance at Christian festivals.[34]

> The Church of England bases a significant part of its identity on its physical presence in every community, and on a 'come to us' strategy. But as community becomes more complex, mere geographical presence is no longer a guarantee that we can connect. The reality is that mainstream culture no longer brings people to the church door. We can no longer assume that we can automatically reproduce ourselves, because the pool of people who regard church as relevant or important is decreasing with every generation.[35]

John Finney's research, *Finding Faith Today*, showed that:

> The most important evangelistic work of the minister appears to be not in the church and the pulpit but in two other kinds of relationships: one-to-one meetings with non-Christians and the 'lapsed' [and] group situations, particularly those where there is an opportunity to talk about the nature of faith.[36]

His survey of recent converts found that only 4% said evangelistic events were the main factor, with a further 13% saying they were a supporting factor.

There are 300,000 Mirpuri people in the UK from the Azad Kashmir region of Pakistan. There is no Mirpuri church. This is one of the largest unreached people groups in the world and they are right on our doorstep. So why is the UK church not throwing resources into evangelism among Mirpuris? No doubt there are many reasons. But perhaps one is the assumption that they are not our mission field. Some people, imbibing the spirit of the age, question whether we should evangelize people of other religions at all. Evangelicals may not think this, but perhaps unconsciously we assume that we are called to reach people we somehow regard as 'dormant' Christians. Stuart Murray says, 'Arguing we should not evangelise other faith communities implies that we should evangelise only "latent Christians" and that evangelism is unpleasant – both concepts deeply rooted in Christendom thinking.'[37]

A newer feature of a Christendom approach is the outsourcing to 'faith communities' of government services. Christian involvement in social action has a long and honourable tradition.[38] But more recently 'faith communities' are being paid by governments to provide charitable services. This is promoted both by the church and by a state keen to reduce the size of the government. The danger, however, is that this becomes a new way in which the church becomes an arm of the state. Along the way, its dependence on state funding with its attendant requirements may blunt the church's prophetic role and evangelistic proclamation. This is not an argument against the practice, but it is a call for us to be alert to the inherent dangers.

Reaching the 40 million

As we have seen, *70% of the UK population have no intention of attending a church service.* This adds up to over 40 million people. In the United States the figure is approximately 85 million.

That of course means that 30% of the UK population attend church occasionally or are open to doing so in the future.

That's a lot of people – nearly 20 million. So the Christendom models still have plenty of mileage in them. We are not suggesting that churches shut down Alpha and Christianity Explored courses, guest services, Sunday schools and so on. Many churches will see gospel fruit from such activities for years to come. We praise God for these opportunities and rejoice when churches work effectively to reach such people.

But how will we reach the 40 million? Or the 85 million? These are critical questions because these numbers are only going to increase.

Anecdotally, church leaders recognize that we are largely reaching people on the fringe or the open de-churched. People are 'returning' to church. Research by John Finney in the 1990s showed three-quarters of those coming to faith were from de-churched backgrounds.[39] But the number of people who will return to church in the future is dwindling all the time.

Consider attendance at Sunday school. In the UK in 1900 it was 55%. By 1940 it was 35%. By 1970 it had dropped to 14%. In 2000 it was just 4%. If the current trend continues, this will drop to only 1 in 100 by 2016. One in 7 forty-year-olds went to Sunday school, which means that only 1 in 7 forty-year-olds might return to church. And in the future the number of potential returnees will dwindle to 1 in 20 and then 1 in 100. Penny Frank of the Church Pastoral Aid Society talks about this being 'the last generation for the Church'. She adds that, as a result, 'children in some of our estates will never cross the bridge to church attendance'.[40] Ninety-six per cent of children in the UK are growing up without any exposure to the church or its message. None of them will ever 'return' to church! They might of course *come* to church for the first time, but they will not *return* to church. Attracting returnees cannot be a strategy for the future. The *Mission-Shaped Church* report concludes:

The sober reality is that we do most of our evangelism, and even
our church planting, among the 30 percent nearest to us – the fringe
and open de-churched. But the stark question remains: what of our
mission to the remaining 60 percent of the nation? Any apostolic
church that derives its nature from the apostolic (or sending)
character of God has no option but to face its mission to the
non-churched, even if this is at the cost of finding new ways of being
and doing church to exist alongside what we do and are at present.
*The task is to become church for them, among them and with them, and under the
Spirit of God to lead them to become church in their own culture.*[41]

From attractional events to attractional communities
In Christendom many people attended church, sometimes
by legal constraint, but more often by social constraint. In
this context churches could legitimately speak of faithfully
proclaiming the gospel because each Sunday they had gospel-
centred sermons. This is no longer the case. We cannot claim
to be faithfully proclaiming the gospel to the lost through our
Sunday preaching when most of the lost do not attend church
in the first place. We need to do mission outside church and
church events. This is something we need to *re*cover rather
than *dis*cover, for the modern evangelical movement was
born out of a recognition that the UK was not a Christian
nation and therefore needed to be evangelized outside of
church buildings and services. George Whitefield and John
Wesley preached the gospel in the open air because they were
not welcome in church buildings, and the people they wanted
to reach were not in church.

We cannot rely on business as usual. We cannot have more
of the same. Evangelism must involve a qualitative change
rather than simply a quantitative change. One of the common
assumptions when people fail to turn up to church is that we
need to improve the experience of church gatherings, the

'product'. We need better music, more relevant sermons, multimedia presentations, engaging dramas. Or we need to relocate to pubs, cafés, art centres. We need cool venues with cool people and cool music. The problem with this approach is the assumption that people will come to church if the product is better. But remember, 70% of the UK population have no intention of attending a church service, and these figures are even higher among young people.

It is no good blaming the lost for failing to turn up, or bemoaning the drift of our nation away from Christianity. 'Our persistent "come to us" mind-set suggests that we really believe that people who refuse to come in the front door are beyond the reach of Christ.'[42] But a farmer cannot blame his crops if he fails to sow and reap. Sunday morning in church is the one place where evangelism cannot take place in our generation because the lost are not there – not until we go out to connect with them where they are, where they feel comfortable, on their territory.

We need to do church and mission in the context of everyday life. We must think of church as a community of people who share life, ordinary life. And the bedrock of mission will be ordinary life.

So, an everyday church with an everyday mission.

Strangers and exiles

It is still unusual to experience personal hostility because we are Christians, but we operate in a culture that is indeed hostile to Christianity. Only last week a member of one of our gospel communities told how friends in his rugby club are vitriolic about the Christian faith on their Facebook pages, apparently without sensing any incongruity between this and their friendship towards him. We may not often be persecuted, but we will be marginalized. You know that you are marginalized when a leading politician is not allowed to answer a question about his faith because his press officer says, 'We don't do God.' Or when a nurse is suspended for praying for a patient's recovery. You know that you are marginalized when a Christian carer is struck off the foster care register for allowing a Muslim girl she's looking after to convert to Christianity. Faith in our culture is allowed to be privately engaging, but it is excluded from public life.

We really need to wake up to the fact that Christians live at the margins. Our society has no time for the message of Jesus, and our allegiance to Jesus as Lord puts us on a collision course with the priorities of the culture. 'Being on the margins rather than in the centre will require a change of perspective, a very different mindset.'[43]

Strangers

Peter opens his first letter by describing his readers as 'God's elect, strangers in the world, scattered throughout Pontus, Galatia, Cappadocia, Asia and Bithynia'. The idea that Christians are 'strangers in the world' is a key motif in the whole letter. Peter calls his readers 'strangers' or 'foreigners' in 1:1 and 1:17, and 'aliens and strangers' in 2:11.

Christians are like immigrants, foreigners, temporary residents, refugees. We do not belong. We do not have the rights of citizens. We are outsiders, living on the edge of the culture.

John Elliott argued that 'strangers' in 1 Peter refers to the social status of Christians before their conversion. They were already outcasts who then found a home among God's people. Elliott's thesis, however, has not persuaded most commentators. 'It underestimates,' argues Miroslav Volf, 'a new estrangement which a Christian way of life creates.'[44] It also ignores the way the terms 'strangers' and 'aliens' were used to describe God's people in the Old Testament (Genesis 23:4; Leviticus 19:34; Psalm 39:12).

In contrast to Elliott, Karen Jobes argues that 'strangers' was a reference to social alienation *after* conversion.[45] She asks how Christians came to be in Asia Minor, a vast, relatively remote area for which we have no evidence of missionary activity in the first century other than the existence of churches in the locations described in 1 Peter 1:1. People have speculated that Peter himself evangelized these regions, hence the association that leads him to write this letter. But again there is no evidence for this. Jobes instead suggests that the Christians were converted elsewhere and then moved to Asia Minor where, no doubt, they continued to spread the message and gain new converts.

Jobes cites the Roman policy of colonizing conquered regions by moving people to new locations. The emperor Claudius is known to have colonized Asia Minor in this way, establishing formal Roman colonies in all the five areas mentioned in 1:1. Non-citizens were sent to such regions, sometimes because they were perceived to be troublemakers in Rome. The main qualification for such deportation was that you lacked Roman citizenship, and the Latin equivalent of 'foreigner' in 1:1 was a legal term referring to a free person who was not a Roman citizen. So such people were perceived as foreigners in the Roman areas from which they were sent *and* in the colonized areas to which they were sent. The most famous Roman expulsion occurred during the reign of Claudius when he expelled the Jews from Rome, including Priscilla and Aquila (Acts 18:2). Among these Jews were Christian converts, perhaps disproportionately so. Many might well have found themselves in Asia Minor where they continued to proclaim the gospel and establish churches. Moreover, there is a long tradition of Peter being based in

Rome long before his later death under Nero. So Peter would have had personal contact with the Christians who were then deported in this way, which would explain why he later writes to them in Asia Minor. Peter may have escaped the expulsion of Jews or, like Priscilla and Aquila (Romans 16:3), returned after the death of Claudius. His cryptic reference to 'Babylon' in 5:13 might be because he did not want to reveal his current location in Rome.

Jobes does not claim that this socio-political background negates a metaphorical understanding of the term. Rather, the two interrelate: 'Peter uses the socio-historical situation of his readers to explain their socio-political situation.'[46] Peter is not saying that it is *as if* his readers are on the margins of society. His readers really *are* on the margins of society.

Whatever the merits of Jobes' historical reconstruction, the important point is that the terms 'aliens' and 'strangers' describe real, social realities. Rather than understanding 'strangers' 'as describing the believer's transitory life on this earth as a journey toward their heavenly home, it should be understood primarily as defining the relationship between the Christian and unbelieving society'.[47] Peter uses their experience of social marginalization to describe their experience in Christ. Miroslav Volf concludes:

> That the members of the Petrine community might have become Christians because many of them were socially marginalized seems an intelligent hypothesis. That they became alienated from their social environment in a new way when they became Christians is what the epistle explicitly states.[48]

Ask the British Home Office how you become a citizen of the UK and they will tell you that you must live in the UK for five years, be of good character and pass a citizenship test.

Except, of course, that there is an easier way, namely, to be born British. That's the way most people become citizens. It was the same in Rome. Some people could earn citizenship, but most were born as citizens.

It is the same for Christians too. We are foreigners and exiles because we have been born anew into a new homeland.

> Praise be to the God and Father of our Lord Jesus Christ! In his great mercy he has given us new birth into a living hope through the resurrection of Jesus Christ from the dead, and into an inheritance that can never perish, spoil or fade – kept in heaven for you.
> (1:3–4)

Peter emphasizes that we have been born *into* something: a living hope and a new inheritance. We have become citizens of a new homeland, not something we earned through good character or by passing a citizenship test, but by being born again.

Peter is not saying that heaven is our new home. Our home is the new creation which is 'kept' in heaven for us. Our inheritance is kept for us (1:4) and we are kept for our inheritance (1:5).

Many of the refugees with whom we work in Sheffield have no certainty of returning to their homeland. Indeed, most of them have no reason to suppose that they will ever go home and every reason to think they will not. But Christians are certain of going home to receive our inheritance, through the resurrection. Jesus has returned home ahead of us, opening up the way (1:3). So we may be strangers now on earth, but we are not strangers in God's kingdom. And the reverse is also true: being members of another kingdom makes us outsiders here on earth.

In 4:4 Peter says that former friends 'think it strange that

you do not plunge with them into the same flood of dissipa-
tion, and they heap abuse on you'. We have become strangers
because we have become strange! Our values, lifestyle, priorities are radically different from those of the surrounding
culture. Our faith makes us strangers in our own land.

Exiles

In his opening description of his readers Peter not only refers
to them as 'strangers', but literally 'strangers of the Diaspora'.
'Foreigners in exile' we might say. As a noun 'Diaspora' was
a technical term for Jews scattered beyond Palestine after the
Babylonian exile in 587 BC. Peter's readers almost certainly
include Gentile Christians, but he likens them to Jews in the
Babylonian exile.

Peter seems to be writing in the style of a Jewish 'Diaspora
letter', a letter written from Jerusalem to Jewish exiles.[49]
Indeed, there are good reasons to think that his letter is
modelled on a letter the prophet Jeremiah wrote back in the
sixth century BC to the exiles in Babylon in Jeremiah 29. This
letter is introduced thus: 'This is the text of the letter that the
prophet Jeremiah sent from Jerusalem to the surviving elders
among the exiles and to the priests, the prophets and all the
other people Nebuchadnezzar had carried into exile from
Jerusalem to Babylon' (29:1). 1 Peter 2:11–12 and Peter's
quote from Psalm 34 in 3:11 seem to echo Jeremiah's call
to 'seek the peace and prosperity of the city to which I have
carried you into exile' (Jeremiah 29:7). Psalm 34 is itself a
psalm of exile. The Greek version of the Old Testament used
by Peter describes God in verse 4 as delivering David from all
'his sojournings', a noun which is related to the word 'aliens'
that Peter uses to describe Christians.

But here is the key thing. At the end of the letter Peter
sends greetings 'from Babylon' (5:13) – almost certainly a

cryptic reference to Rome. This is not a letter from home in Jerusalem to exiles in Babylon. This is a letter *from* exile *to* exile, for exile is not geographically defined. Christians are strangers because their identity has so radically changed that they are no longer at home in the country of their birth. The reference to Babylon reminds us of Daniel who rose to the top of the Babylonian political system, fulfilling Jeremiah's call to seek the prosperity of the city. We are called to get involved in the world and to bless our cities. But we cannot do so on the basis that our nation is a Christian nation. This is not our home.

Hostility

Peter says that his readers 'may have had to suffer grief in all kinds of trials' (1:6). Commentators agree that the suffering Peter's readers were undergoing was not at this point state-sponsored imprisonment or martyrdom (though these would come later). Instead it was the suspicion and censure of their neighbours. Karen Jobes says, 'Because of their Christian faith, they were being marginalized by their society, alienated in their relationships, and threatened with – if not experiencing – a loss of honour and socio-economic standing (and possibly worse).'[50] Howard Marshall says,

> At this stage it seems that state action was rare . . . and that what Christians had to fear was more in the nature of social ostracism, unfriendly acts by neighbours, pressure on Christian wives from pagan husbands, masters taking it out on Christian slaves and other actions of that kind. It was sufficient, in any case, to make life uncomfortable.[51]

The hostility described throughout the letter is verbal slander and malicious accusations: 'they accuse you of doing wrong

. . . the ignorant talk of foolish men . . . insult . . . those who speak maliciously against your good behaviour in Christ . . . slander' (2:12, 15; 3:9, 16). 'It was precisely the precarious legal status of foreigners that provided the closest analogy to the kind of treatment Christians could expect from the hostile culture in which they lived.'[52] We cannot know what people said to Christians in the marketplace and street. Day-to-day insults are rarely written down in the historical records. However, there is a famous piece of graffiti surviving from the first century which depicts a donkey on a cross with the words: 'Alexander worships his God.' Alexander, it seems, was a Christian whose faith in a crucified Saviour was being ridiculed. Christians were being slandered, excluded and marginalized. In other words, it was much like our experience today.

An unseen Lord

In 1:8 Peter says of Jesus: 'Though you have not seen him, you love him; and even though you do not see him now, you believe in him and are filled with an inexpressible and glorious joy.' We love what we have not seen. We believe in what we cannot see.

Peter recognizes that this will be received with incredulity by our unbelieving neighbours. The Roman Empire knew how to do propaganda, and how to project its glory and power on its subjects. Symbols of power were everywhere: Roman standards, eagles, magnificent civic buildings. Everywhere the eye turned in the cities of Asia Minor there were signs of the triumph of Roman imperialism. The eternal city was setting itself up for an eternal reign.

It is not so very different today. We still use Romanesque architecture and symbols to express imperial power. Eagles or lions adorn our currency. Civic buildings boast

Roman columns and domes. But the power that projects itself with the greatest ubiquity is that of consumerism. Everywhere the eye turns in Western cities we see advertising, brands, logos, hoardings. It is impossible to avoid them. So it is hardly surprising that such values are implanted in our lives.

All the time, Christians orientate their lives to a Lord they cannot see. Peter knows that this is a hard thing to explain to people. We shape our lives around something we cannot see and have never seen. Peter recognizes that it makes us sound weird.

A rejected Lord

Peter says,

> Concerning this salvation, the prophets, who spoke of the grace that
> was to come to you, searched intently and with the greatest care,
> trying to find out the time and circumstances to which the Spirit
> of Christ in them was pointing when he predicted the sufferings of
> Christ and the glories that would follow.
>
> (1:10)

The message of the Old Testament is that of the sufferings of Christ and the glories that would follow. Jesus sets the pattern: suffering followed by glory. Indeed Jesus suffered the ultimate marginalization: he was pushed out of the world on to the cross. As Jesus said, 'If the world hates you, keep in mind that it hated me first . . . If they persecuted me, they will persecute you also' (John 15:18–20). Or consider the words of Hebrews:

> The high priest carries the blood of animals into the Most Holy Place
> as a sin offering, but the bodies are burned outside the camp. And

so Jesus also suffered outside the city gate to make the people holy
through his own blood. Let us, then, go to him outside the camp,
bearing the disgrace he bore. For here we do not have an enduring
city, but we are looking for the city that is to come.
(Hebrews 13:11–14)

We have become outsiders just as Jesus was an outsider. We
are marginal in our culture because Jesus is marginal. The
cross is the ultimate expression of marginalization, and to
follow Jesus is to take up our cross daily, daily to experience
marginalization and hostility. Being on the margins is normal
Christian experience. Christendom was the aberration. Rather
than assume we should have a voice in the media or on the
high street, we need to regain the sense that anything other
than persecution is an unexpected bonus.

But Peter also says, '[We] have been chosen according
to the foreknowledge of God the Father' (1:2). And just as
we share in Christ's suffering so we will share in 'the glories
that would follow' (1:11; 4:12–13). God has chosen us for a
purpose. 'Out of all nations you will be my treasured pos-
session,' he says to his people. 'Although the whole earth
is mine, you will be for me a kingdom of priests and a holy
nation' (Exodus 19:5–6). The doctrine of election, God's
choice of us, is never intended as an indulgence. Its purpose
is always mission.

And we can not only survive on the margins, we can thrive.
From the margins we point to God's coming world and offer
an alternative lifestyle, alternative values and relationships – a
community which proves incredibly attractive. 1 Peter equips
us to go back into the world, into our classrooms, board-
rooms, factories, playgrounds, changing rooms as men and
women who, like our Saviour before us, can be marginal yet
truly world-changing.

2. EVERYDAY COMMUNITY

1 Peter 1:13 – 2:8

Imagine you woke up one day to discover that you were a missionary in a foreign land. The language, culture, worldview and values are all unfamiliar. Fortunately you are part of a team. What are you going to do? Together you are going to learn the language and culture. You are going to explore how the Bible story interacts with the outlook of the people around you. You are going to try to connect with them at a relational level.

This is the situation in which the church in the West finds itself. The culture has moved on. As we've already seen, it is not what it was a hundred years ago when it was significantly shaped by the Bible story. We are in a missionary situation. We cannot continue to undertake mission in a pastoral mode. We cannot assume people feel any need or obligation to attend church. We cannot even assume we understand the culture. We need to operate as missionaries in a foreign land.

We cannot expect the world to be like us

A Christendom mentality expects the world to be like us and share our values. And it protests when the world is not like us. Often Christians complain about the treatment of Christianity in the wider culture. They bemoan legislation that does not reflect Christian values. They lament the representation of Christianity in the media. They decry politicians who profess themselves atheists. We do not welcome any of these developments. But none of them surprise us. We cannot expect the world to be like us. Indeed we are surprised whenever we *do* see the culture conforming to Christian values or reacting positively to the church. This is perhaps something the Free churches can teach the Anglicans in England. Part of our story is persecution and marginalization. We are not part of the Establishment, and often in our history we have been persecuted by the Establishment. Anglicanism often lacks this collective memory. It really is a surprise to Anglicans to find themselves marginalized because they are used to being part of the Establishment. Yet often the Free churches have sought to suppress this memory, seeking respectability. Many of the grand Nonconformist chapels built on the high street were an attempt to say, 'We've arrived; we're part of mainstream society.' The tradition of non-conformist dissent has been replaced by middle-class conformity. We need to discover or recover the sense that if this year we are not imprisoned, then it has been a good year in which by the grace of God we have got off lightly.

It was ever thus. In 2:4–8 Peter says that believers are 'like living stones' 'being built into a spiritual house' with Jesus as the cornerstone or capstone. We are living stones like

Christ the living Stone. But notice how Christ the Stone is described. He is 'rejected by men but chosen by God and precious to him' (2:4). He is 'the stone the builders rejected [which] has become the capstone' (2:7). He is the 'stone that causes men to stumble' (2:8). Peter is following Jesus himself in using Psalm 118:22 to describe his rejection by humanity (Mark 12:10). Jesus is rejected by people, but chosen by God.

The cornerstone is the stone to which all the other stones are aligned. The Stone to which we as living stones are aligned is the Stone that has been rejected by human beings, but is honoured by God. So we can expect human rejection and divine honour to be our experience as well. Indeed Peter says, '"Whoever believes in him will not be put to shame". So the honour is for you who believe' (2:6–7 ESV).

It is not our culture any more

In Christendom we could assume that the culture of the church was similar to the culture of the world. Or we could at least claim that it should be. Some individuals might reject the values and worldview of the church, but the culture as a whole was congruent with Christianity. To some extent this worked in both directions. The church could claim that the world should match the culture of the church. But at the same time the church conformed to the culture of the world. This is a Christendom mentality.

We can no longer assume that the wider culture matches that of the church or that people share a similar worldview to ours. Most people do not believe in a personal God and most people do not believe there is only one true religion. People are biblically illiterate. We cannot talk about guilt, faith, religion or even God, and assume that people understand what we are talking about. 'The gospel used to have more plausibility structures supporting it than it does today,'[1] says Randy

Newman. We cannot talk about Jesus and assume that people locate him in a framework of creation, fall, redemption and future hope. Everything has to be explained. Stuart Murray relates:

> In a London school a teenager with no church connections hears the Christmas story for the first time. His teacher tells it well and he is fascinated by this amazing story. Risking his friends' mockery, after the lesson he thanks her for the story. One thing had disturbed him, so he asks: 'Why did they give the baby a swear word for his name?'

> One Sunday in Oxford a man visits a church building to collect something for his partner who works during the week in a creative-arts project the church runs. He arrives as the morning congregation is leaving and recognizes the minister, whom he knows. Surprised, he asks: 'What are all these people doing here? I didn't know churches were open on Sundays!'[2]

These are extreme cases, but they illustrate the growing disconnection between Christianity and our culture. Historian Callum Brown says,

> What is taking place is not merely the continued decline of organized Christianity, but the death of the culture that formerly conferred Christian identity upon the British people as a whole. If a core identity survives for Britons, it is certainly no longer Christian. The culture of Christianity has gone in the Britain of the new millennium.[3]

Many people, for example, in our urban UK context are a strange hybrid of secularism and pluralism. They themselves have grown up without any meaningful church contact, but now live in a neighbourhood with many Muslims. They believe about religions what we believe about denominations: there are real differences, but fundamentally we are all the same. I, Tim, have had a number of conversations in which I talked about faith in Jesus and my friends talked about 'being religious'. They assume we are calling them to be religious – not in the sense of law-based religious activity or morality, but in a more general sense of a vague spiritual sensibility which they are free to interpret for themselves. Simply to call such people to faith in Christ as their Saviour is meaningless. They do not know who Christ is, what faith is, why they need saving, or from what they need saving. They would probably interpret it as a call to neighbour-love and private prayer. Tim Keller says,

> In the past, many of our neighbours could understand traditional Christian preaching even when they responded with disagreement or indifference. During the last fifteen years, however, our message is increasingly met with dumbfounded incomprehension or outrage. Until a generation ago in the US, most adults had similar moral intuitions whether they were born-again believers, church-goers, nominal Christians, or non-believers. That has changed.[4]

Claiming that the West is a mission field is now common. But there is a big gap between the rhetoric and the reality of our attitudes. One of the measures of that gap is the extent to which we are willing – or unwilling – to learn from the experience of mission and the church around the world. If we really believed we were in a mission field then we would all be reading books written by Third-World Christians and cross-cultural missionaries.

Let us give one example. Chronological Bible storying is an approach to pioneer evangelism and church planting that is commonly used among unreached people groups around the world.[5] Missionaries take time to understand the culture and then create a set of Bible stories that cover the key turning points in the story of salvation, along with Bible stories that address the barriers and bridges to belief in that culture. They then teach these stories to those who are interested. People learn the stories so that they can retell them and also reflect on them together. Typically there are thirty to forty stories in a story set, and they climax with the death and resurrection of Christ. Those who are interested continue with stories in Acts to help form new believers into churches. Different story sets can also be used in discipleship and leadership training. In this way even non-literate peoples gain a good understanding of the Bible.

This approach is widely used in many varied cultures around the world. Yet its use in the West is rare.[6] Why is this? Where it has been used, it has actually been successful. I once talked to a member of a church planting team in Birmingham who told me how valuable storying was proving with her Muslim contacts. In the same conversation she asked how she could reach the disaffected white teenagers in her church youth group. I told her how effective storying had been in engaging young people in our context. It was a eureka moment for her. She had never thought to use storying with Westerners. Among those leading the development and deployment of chronological Bible storying has been the International Board of Mission of the Southern Baptist Convention. I once asked a student in an SBC Bible college whether storying was taught or used in churches in the southern United States. He laughed. Our point is not to push storying (though that would be no bad thing) but to highlight the extent to which, despite our rhetoric, we do not see our context as a missionary context.

Peter does not present a complex model of how we should adapt to our context. Instead he describes the new identity of his readers in a way that inevitably shapes their engagement with their neighbours in a gospel-centred way. At a number of key moments, Peter says 'Therefore' in a way that turns identity into action, indicatives into imperatives (1:13; 2:1; 4:1, 7). There are repeated references to the 'walk' of Christians (1:15, 17, 18; 2:12; 3:1, 2, 16). 1 Peter shows how our new identity as the people of God enables us to live on the margins.

So the 'strangers' motif is more than just descriptive. It also suggests how Peter's readers are to relate to an alien culture. Think of your own encounters with another culture, on holiday or mission visits perhaps. Think how you related. As foreigners Christians are to treat their 'host' culture with respect, honour those in authority and seek its prosperity. But we will never really feel at home in the culture.

Peter highlights the need for 'respect' or 'honour' to everyone, including those in political authority, towards wives in the home and towards enquirers, however hostile they may be in their intent (2:17, 18; 3:7, 15). His hearers are to show 'fear' to masters in the workplace and husbands in the home (2:18; 3:1).

Think of a diplomat. Her ultimate allegiance is to her homeland, but she pursues the cause of her homeland by showing meticulous respect for the culture and people of the country to which she has been assigned. Although we have been distanced from our previous culture by our new birth, we pursue the cause of our new King by showing respect to the people around us.

> But in your hearts set apart Christ as Lord. Always be prepared to give an answer to everyone who asks you to give the reason for the hope that you have. But do this with gentleness and respect, keeping a clear conscience, so that those who speak maliciously against your good behaviour in Christ may be ashamed of their slander.
> (3:15–16)

We set apart Christ as Lord because our homeland has changed. We proclaim the gospel to extend the rule of our Lord. But we do this with 'gentleness and respect' to confound our accusers.

Citing Peter's call for 'gentleness' (3:4, 15), Croatian theologian Miroslav Volf argues for what he calls 'soft difference': 'Fear for oneself and one's identity creates hardness. The difference that joins itself with hardness always presents the other with a choice: either submit or be rejected.' By contrast:

> . . . for people who live the soft difference, mission fundamentally takes the form of witness and invitation. They seek to win others without pressure or manipulation . . . The soft difference is the missionary side of following in the footsteps of the crucified Messiah. It is not an optional extra, but part and parcel of Christian identity itself.[7]

Rediscovering the culture

Recognizing our missionary context means we can no longer assume that the church understands the culture. We need to rediscover or relearn the culture. We need to get to know our neighbourhood, its people, their stories, values, worldview and culture. We need to ask the kind of questions that missionaries ask when they enter a new culture, questions such as:

Where?
- Where are the places and activities in which you can meet people ('the missional spaces')?
- Where do people experience community?
- Are there existing social networks with which we can engage, or do we need to find ways of creating community within a neighbourhood?
- *Where* should you be to have missional opportunities?

When?

- What are the patterns and timescales of your neighbourhood ('the missional rhythms')?
- When are the times when you can connect with people ('the missional moments')?
- How do people organize their time?
- What cultural experiences and celebrations do people value? How might these be used as bridges to the gospel?
- *When* should you be available to have missional opportunities?

What?

- What are people's fears, hopes and hurts?
- What 'gospel' stories are told in the neighbourhood? What gives people identity (creation)? How do they account for wrong in the world (fall)? What is their solution (redemption)? What are their hopes (consummation)?
- What are the barrier beliefs or assumptions that cause people to dismiss the gospel?
- What sins will the gospel first confront and heal?
- In what ways are people self-righteous?
- What is the good news for people in this neighbourhood?
- What will church look like for people in this neighbourhood?

Communities are not always defined by geography. They may also be defined by ethnicity, leisure interest, time of life and so on. In an urban context most people are part of several overlapping communities.

Ask people what it's like to live in your area. If you are an insider, ask outsiders what they find weird about your community. If you are an outsider, ask insiders how they view their community.

You might ask these kinds of questions on first encountering a new community or neighbourhood. But they should also be questions we ask all the time so that missional reflection becomes a normal part of our lives. We cannot work on our understanding of our neighbourhood and then sign it off. These questions should be part of ongoing discussions.

Organize activities such as team meetings, one-to-one mentoring, talk preparation and readings in public spaces such as cafés, pubs and parks. This will help you to think in a missional way as you plan and prepare. If you prepare Bible teaching in a coffee shop, for example, you are more likely to find yourself developing your teaching as a dialogue with the culture. But if you simply prepare in your study surrounded by your books, then you will naturally speak into this context, addressing the concerns of professional exegetes. If you hold a leaders' meeting in a café then you are more likely to think in missional terms as you discuss the business of the church.

In many cases you will be able to identify where community happens in your neighbourhood and therefore become part of that community. The church often seems to have an obsession with doing everything itself. If you want to reach hikers, you start a church hiking group. But why not join an *existing* hiking group? Somebody else does all the hard work of organizing the group. There may, though, be situations in which you discover there is no real community going on. Then you can become the people who bring others together.

Loving the culture

Some of Peter's readers may have responded to hostility with passivity – maintaining a low profile, keeping quiet about their Lord and conforming to social patterns as much as possible. The equivalent today are those who would hide in a ghetto or reshape Christianity into more socially acceptable forms. Others may have responded with aggression, wanting to fight back. The equivalent today are those would assert the Christian-ness of the nation and fight for Christian values to be normative within society.

Peter charts a third route: doing good in suffering – what we might call 'proactive gentleness'. Christians are not to become a sectarian ghetto. Instead they are repeatedly called upon to respond to hostility with good works (2:12, 15, 20, 24; 3:1, 11, 13, 17; 4:19), an echo of Jeremiah's call to the exiles in Babylon which we have already seen: 'Seek the peace and prosperity of the city to which I have carried you into exile. Pray to the LORD for it, because if it prospers, you too will prosper' (Jeremiah 29:7). There is even an element of self-interest. Jeremiah warns the exiles that return is not imminent so they should seek the prosperity of the city because, for the time being, it is also their prosperity.

We need to love the city. Tim Keller identifies the following characteristics of a missional church:[8]

> A 'missional' small group is not necessarily one which is doing
> some kind of specific 'evangelism' programme (though that is to be
> recommended). Rather:
> 1. If its members love and talk positively about the city and
>   neighbourhood
> 2. If they speak in language that is not filled with pious tribal
>   or technical terms and phrases, nor disdainful and embattled
>   language
> 3. If in their Bible study they apply the gospel to the core concerns
>   and stories of the people of the culture
> 4. If they are obviously interested in and engaged with the literature

and art and thought of the surrounding culture and can discuss it both appreciatively and yet critically

5. If they exhibit deep concern for the poor and generosity with their money and purity and respect with regard to opposite sex, and show humility toward people of other races and cultures

6. If they do not bash other Christians and churches

. . . *then* seekers and non-believing people from the city (a) will be invited and (b) will come and will stay as they explore spiritual issues. If these marks are not there it will only be able to include believers or traditional, 'Christianized' people.

It is so important to love your neighbourhood and its culture. As we sense our growing marginalization with the wider culture it is all too easy to view it as a threat. But this is not a good starting point for reaching people with the gospel. A while back I, Tim, did some research on small groups and visited a number of small-group Bible studies. In two cases the group began to speak of Muslims in their neighbourhood. Their language suggested that they felt they were embattled with Muslims poised to 'take over'. It turned out that no-one had talked to Muslim neighbours at all. Muslims had become a dehumanized 'other'. This attitude rendered relationship-building for the sake of the gospel all but impossible.

You might like to consider how your church community measures up against Keller's criteria. Keller says that the members of a missional community 'love and talk positively about the city and neighbourhood'. You might like to invite your missional community to identify ten things you all love about your neighbourhood.

In our context we have woven a commitment to 'blessing the city' into our values. We say:

We are committed to blessing our neighbourhoods and cities
– redressing injustice, pursuing reconciliation and welcoming
the marginalized. We celebrate the diversity of cultures in our
local contexts while recognising the need for gospel renewal. We
encourage one another to glorify God and serve others through the
workplace, business, community projects, government and artistic
endeavour.[9]

Chosen to be distinctive

But alongside Peter's call for positive engagement and respect
is a negative counter-side. Peter calls on his readers to abstain
from sinful desires: 'As obedient children, do not conform to
the evil desires you had when you lived in ignorance' (1:14), and
'Dear friends, I urge you, as aliens and strangers in the world,
to abstain from sinful desires, which war against your soul'
(2:11; see also 1:18; 4:2–3). This act of abstaining from sinful
desires will bring Christians into conflict with a culture that
does not restrain sinful desires (4:2–4). Our imagined diplomat's ultimate loyalty is to her homeland. So she will adapt and
adopt local customs, but only insofar as they are compatible
and congruent with the values of her homeland. Karen Jobes
says that Peter presents 'the challenging principle that it is
better to suffer than to sin'. 'First Peter challenges Christians to
re-examine our acceptance of society's norms and to be willing
to suffer the alienation of being a visiting foreigner in our own
culture wherever its values conflict with those of Christ.'[10]

Having described Christians as strangers and exiles in 1:1,
Peter says we 'have been chosen according to the foreknowledge of God the Father, through the sanctifying work of the
Spirit, for obedience to Jesus Christ and sprinkling by his
blood' (1:2). Why does Peter say these things in this particular
order? At first sight it seems somewhat random – not the list
we would have put together.

It takes us back to Mount Sinai. God tells Pharaoh to free Israel, 'my firstborn son' (Exodus 4:22–23). God is the Father of Israel who has chosen Israel from among all the nations to know and worship him. And God brings them to Mount Sinai to give them the covenant with the Ten Commandments. There he calls them 'a holy nation' (Exodus 19:4–6). The word 'sanctified' means 'made holy' or 'set apart'. They are called to be distinctive, set apart from all the nations to live under God's reign and so make God known to the nations. God sanctifies them so that there will be one place on earth where the goodness of his reign can be seen. So God's people are saved for missional obedience. The covenant is confirmed by the sprinkling of blood.

> Then [Moses] took the Book of the Covenant and read it to the people. They responded, 'We will do everything the LORD has said; we will obey.'
>
> Moses then took the blood, sprinkled it on the people and said, 'This is the blood of the covenant that the LORD has made with you in accordance with all these words.'
>
> (Exodus 24:7–8)

All these elements are present in 1 Peter 1:2. We are chosen from the world by the Father, sanctified for the world by the Spirit and called to missional obedience by the sprinkling of Christ's blood.

Peter identifies the church as the new Israel (1:2, 18–19; 2:9–10). We are recapitulating the story of Israel. And Peter locates us in that story at Mount Sinai. Israel at Sinai were strangers going to a homeland or an inheritance they had never seen, kept en route by the pillars of cloud and fire. In the same way we are strangers going to an inheritance we have never seen, kept en route by the Holy Spirit (1:3–5). And like

Israel we are chosen to be distinctive through obedience to God so that the world can see that God is good (1:2; 2:9–12).

In 1:15–16 Peter says: 'But just as he who called you is holy, so be holy in all you do; for it is written: "Be holy, because I am holy."' Peter is quoting from Leviticus. Leviticus can be a scary book, full of rules and regulations with which we find it hard to connect. But fundamentally it is about God creating a new society through his Word which is distinctive in every way. They will display the holiness of God in a way that attracts the nations to find blessing in God as God promised to Abraham. Leviticus is intended to create this distinctive people by shaping every aspect of their lives, individually and corporately. It was not just about what people did in the temple; it was about what they did in the market. This holiness knows no boundaries. It defines our friendships, marriages, work, leisure, finances and politics. Holiness is as much about what you do on a Monday morning on the factory floor as it is about what you do on a Sunday morning in a church gathering. Holiness is as much about the kind of neighbour you are as it is about the kind of church member you are. It is as much about who you are when you are holding a steering wheel as who you are when you are holding a Bible. Like Leviticus, Peter is going to spell out what it means for the church to be distinctive in every area of life, but the headline is: 'Be holy, because I am holy.' 'Be distinctive, because I am distinctive.'

We cannot expect to be like the world
An event-based approach to evangelism which is characteristic of a Christendom mentality is constantly trying to create experiences that match those found in the world. We want our music, our oratory, our style to be such that people will be drawn to our meetings.

But it is a mistake to pursue relevance as an end in itself

or to emphasize how we are like the world around us. For one thing, our 'product' will always be inferior to that offered by Hollywood, Facebook and Nintendo. Brits spend twenty hours a week watching television, Americans twenty-eight hours. We are entertained by multi-million-dollar movies. We engage in sophisticated role-play and action computer games. 'We are naïve to think the church can compete with these stimuli through three songs and a thirty-minute sermon or drama and a worship band.'[11] We simply cannot compete on entertainment.

At best this distracts us from the need to create distinctive communities that communicate a distinctive gospel, a gospel which more often than not grates with the wider culture. At worst the medium becomes the message, and the challenge of the gospel is lost among the entertainment or watered down to make it palatable. We have already seen that in a post-Christian context we cannot rely on church events, however cool, because the majority of people will not attend. Now we see another reason not to focus on 'relevant' events. Our missional cutting edge is not events that are *like* the culture, but a life and message that are *unlike* the culture.

Trying to match the world begs the question: If the church is like the world then why bother with the church? The more we become like the world, the less we have to offer. Certainly we will want to avoid unnecessary offence and an off-putting experience. But what will draw people to church is always going to be what is *different* about us. Says Lois Barrett,

> The church as an alternative community can make a powerful witness when it chooses to live differently from the dominant society at just a few key points. An important task of the church is to discern what are those key points at which to be different from the evil of the world.[12]

So difference is what we need to pursue. But this does not mean being gratuitously different. We can certainly put people off by being culturally weird, dated or obscure. Nevertheless we will only attract people through gospel distinctiveness. We become relevant to our world only by being gospel-centred. Os Guinness says:

> By our uncritical pursuit of relevance we have actually courted irrelevance; by our breathless chase after relevance without a matching commitment to faithfulness, we have become not only unfaithful but irrelevant; by our determined efforts to redefine ourselves in ways that are more compelling to the modern world than are faithful to Christ, we have lost not only our identity but our authority and our relevance.[13]

Even if we could produce cool church events, we would create a generation of Christian consumers who look to the church to entertain them. It would only create a consumer-mentality among churchgoers. We would soon have a generation of Christians who move from church to church, hunting experiences. Some churches would attract those who want an intellectual experience through good teaching; others would attract Christians who want an emotional experience through good corporate worship. But there would be little sense in local churches that 'each member belongs to all the others' (Romans 12:5).

People often ask us what our meetings are like in The Crowded House. We have taken to refusing to answer that question if we can get away with it because it misses the point of what we are trying to do. We are not proposing a formula for better meetings. In fact, our meetings are very ordinary. The teaching and music are OK, but nothing special. If you visited you would probably be disappointed.

At the heart of our vision is not a new way of doing events, but the creation of Word-centred gospel communities in which people are sharing life with one another and with unbelievers, seeking to bless their neighbourhoods, 'gospelling' one another and sharing the good news with unbelievers. The context for this gospel-centred community and mission is not events, but ordinary, everyday life.

Programmes are what we create when Christians are not doing what they are supposed to be doing in everyday life. Because we are not pastoring one another in everyday life we create accountability groups. Because we are not sharing the gospel in everyday life we create guest services. Because we are not joining social groups to witness to Jesus we create our own church social groups. Please do not misunderstand. We are not against meetings or events or programmes. Indeed the regular meeting of the church around God's Word is vital for the health of everything else, for this is where God's people are prepared for works of service. But the works of service themselves take place in the context of everyday life.

Differentiated engagement

Richard Niebuhr famously suggested five contrasting Christian attitudes towards culture:[14] (1) Christ against culture; (2) Christ of culture; (3) Christ above culture; (4) Christ and culture in paradox; and (5) Christ transforming culture. Although a useful tool for thinking about the issues, the main problem with Niebuhr's taxonomy is that it assumes an undifferentiated definition of culture. This allows Niebuhr to accuse those within the 'Christ-against-culture' model of being inconsistent: of rejecting civil government (Anabaptists) or fine art (fundamentalists), but adopting other cultural forms such as language, traditional learning and agriculture. But John Howard Yoder, the leading Mennonite theologian, argues that this is precisely what Christians should be doing:

> Some elements of culture the church categorically rejects
> (pornography. tyranny, cultic idolatry). Other dimensions of culture
> it accepts within clear limits (economic production, commerce,
> the graphic arts, paying taxes for peacetime civil government).
> To still other dimensions of culture Christian faith gives a new
> motivation and coherence (agriculture, family life, literacy, conflict
> resolution, empowerment). Still others it strips of their claims to
> possess autonomous truth and value, and uses them as vehicles of
> communication (philosophy, language, Old Testament ritual, music).
> Still other forms of culture are created by the Christian churches
> (hospitals, service of the poor, generalized education).[15]

In other words culture is not a uniform or monolithic entity. It contains within it elements that are good and elements that are bad from a gospel perspective. Being asked to identify with one of Niebuhr's categories is a bit like being asked whether you like movies or how fast you drive your car. It depends on the movie or the road conditions, and it depends on what aspects of culture we are considering. Os Guinness and David Wells say,

> We are to live in the world in a stance of both Yes and No,
> affirmation and antithesis, or of being 'against the world/for the
> world.' This tension is crucial to the faithfulness of the church, and
> to her integrity and effectiveness in the world . . . The Christian
> faith is unashamedly world-affirming, and has a peerless record in
> contributing to education, to philanthropy, to social reforms, to
> medicine, to the rise of science, to the emergence of democracy and
> human rights, as well as to building schools, hospitals, universities,
> orphanages, and other beneficial institutions. Yet at the same time,

the Christian faith is also world-denying, insisting on the place of prophets as well as priests, on sacrifice as well as fulfilment, on the importance of fasts as well as feasts, and on the place for exposing and opposing the world when its attitudes and actions are against the commands of God and the interests of humanity. Not surprisingly, the church's constant temptation has been to relax this tension from one side or the other . . .[16]

Miroslav Volf suggests that Peter's use of the alien and stranger motif allows him to present a differentiated approach to culture. Peter does not want Christians to define their identity simply as difference from the culture – though he calls on them to embrace difference when this arises. Instead he wants them to see themselves in terms of their new identity in Christ. When Peter wants to warn Christians against certain behaviours, 'the force of the injunction is not "Do not be as your neighbours are!" but "Do not be as you were!"' Volf comments:

> When identity is forged primarily through the negative process of the rejection of the beliefs and practices of others . . . we have to push others away from ourselves and keep them at a distance . . . Only those who refuse to be defined by their enemies can bless them.[17]

People often highlight the tension between Peter's calls to resist and to submit. But Peter, argues Volf, is giving 'an example of differentiated acceptance and rejection of the surrounding culture'.

> That is, foreigners dwell respectfully in their host nation but participate in its culture only to the extent that its values and customs coincide with their own that they wish to preserve. In this way the salutation of the letter introduces a concept of differentiated

engagement with society . . . of neither full assimilation nor complete withdrawal.[18]

Tim Keller summarizes:

> Unlike models that call for a transformation of culture or that call for a Christendom-like alliance of church and state, Peter expects the gospel to always be highly offensive, never completely embraced or accepted by the world. This is a caution to those evangelicals and mainline Christians who hope to bring about an essentially Christian culture.
>
> And unlike models that call solely for evangelism and are highly pessimistic about influencing culture, both Peter in 1 Peter 2:12 and Jesus in Matthew 5:16 expect some aspects of Christian faith and practice to be highly attractive in any pagan culture, influencing people to praise and glorify God.[19]

The key distinctive is love

Peter's call to be holy comes to a climax in 1:22: 'Now that you have purified yourselves by obeying the truth so that you have sincere love for your brothers, love one another deeply, from the heart.' We are to be distinctive, and our key distinctive is to be brotherly and sisterly love.

The desire to be part of the 'in crowd', to be accepted, to be an insider is strong within us all. In part this reflects the fact that we are made in the image of the relational God. God is persons-in-community and we too are persons-in-community. So it is no surprise to find that we desire community; it is a good and godly desire.

But the problem is that this desire for community with people can outgrow our desire for community with God. Being accepted by a friendship group or the culture can matter more to us that God's opinion. The Bible calls this 'the fear of man'. Our insecurities make exclusion scary. But in this age some rejection is inevitable for those who follow a crucified Lord. 'May I never boast,' says Paul, 'except in the cross of our Lord Jesus Christ, through which the world has been crucified to me, and I to the world' (Galatians 6:14).

How then can we thrive on the margins? An essential part of the gospel's response is that we are not alone, not even in our marginalization. By being 'in' Christ we are 'in with' his people who, though rejected by the world, are precious to God. Paradoxically, although comprised of the socially insignificant, because of who Christ is, the church is the ultimate 'in crowd'.

It is hard for us to grasp the significance of this community identity because we live in a radically individualistic culture. We bring this worldview with us into the church so that it shapes our understanding of the gospel. So we have a loose connection with Christians on a Sunday, but then largely we go back to living our everyday lives on our own. No wonder we struggle to thrive. Our faith is animated on Sunday mornings as we sing God's praise and hear his Word. But it limps along during the week when we live apart from the body of Christ.

We need to allow the gospel rather than the prevailing secular and socially fragmented story that our society tells to define our identity. In Christ we have been restored to what we were originally made to be: men and women who live in community, characterized by sincere brotherly love. This is what Peter says: 'Now that you have purified yourselves by obeying the truth so that you have sincere love for your brothers, love one another deeply, from the heart' (1:22).

In 1:3 Peter talked about our new birth into a new homeland that makes us strangers and aliens in our culture. In 1:23 Peter again talks about being born anew, but this time we are reborn into *a new family*. The language of family runs through this section of the letter. We are 'children' with God as our 'Father' (1:14, 17). This comes with an obligation to display the family likeness, for we are told to be holy because God is holy (1:16–17). Peter goes on: 'For you know that it was not with perishable things such as silver or gold that you were redeemed from the empty way of life handed down to you from your forefathers, but with the precious blood of Christ, a lamb without blemish or defect' (1:18–19). 'Forefathers' is literally 'fathers'. We have been redeemed from one family tradition into another. Our family background has a big influence on our actions, but we have been set free from a destructive family background.

The two halves of verse 22 are not linked by 'so that' (NIV), but 'for' (ESV): 'Having purified your souls by your obedience to the truth *for* a sincere brotherly love . . .' Brotherly love is not a by-product of purification by obedience to truth; it is its *purpose*. We have been born again *for* brotherly love. The Christian community is not a happy by-product of our salvation, nor a convenient help to individual Christians. We have been saved to be God's holy people, Christ's bride, a new family.

We often understand that Jesus died for us on the cross in very personal terms and celebrate this with songs littered with singular pronouns. And the gospel is certainly not less than this. The Son of God 'loved me and gave himself for me,' says Paul (Galatians 2:20). But the gospel is much more. Christ died for his people, so he could present his bride to himself, radiant and pure. He died so that he could be the second Adam creating a new humanity who are righteous in him. Becoming a Christian is about being born again into a new race.

In 2:1 Peter says, 'Therefore, rid yourselves of all malice

and all deceit, hypocrisy, envy, and slander of every kind.'
You cannot do these sins on your own! They are sins against
other people, the antithesis of love. Instead of 'malice', we are
'to love one another deeply'. Instead of 'deceit' and 'hypocrisy', we are to show 'sincere love' (literally 'un-hypocritical'
love). Instead of 'envy' and 'slander', we are to love another
'from the heart' (2:1; 1:22).

The word translated 'strangers' in 1:1, 17 and 2:11 literally
means 'without house' or 'without home' or 'without family'.
We are 'un-family'. It is the opposite of the word that Peter
uses in 2:5 to talk about 'a spiritual *house*'. Roman society was
viewed as a family with Caesar as the 'Patriarch'. Their new
birth meant Peter's readers had moved outside this family.
They had become outsiders, homeless, un-family. But they
are being built into a spiritual home, a new family (2:5). We
are not called to live as isolated individuals alone on the
margins. We are being built into a new home, born again into
a new family.

Peter is not just talking about a Sunday morning service.
He is talking about living as a community who love one
another sincerely from the heart and are deeply engaged in
one another's lives. He is talking about people you drop in on
on the way back from work. Perhaps because you have had a
bad day and you just want to hang out with people and pray
together. Or perhaps because you have had a great conversation with a neighbour and you want to tell someone about it.

The missional power of everyday community

The Christian community is not only God's survival strategy
for Christians on the margins. The marginalized Christian
community is also God's missionary strategy. We might
imagine that greater impact could be had from the centre
with the ear of the rich and famous and opportunities to exert

influence upon the beautiful and powerful. But God calls us to bring him glory through an everyday community of grace (2:11–12).

So the Christian community demonstrates the effectiveness of the gospel. We are the living proof that the gospel is not an empty word, but a powerful Word that takes men and women who are lovers of self and transforms them by grace through the Spirit into people who love God and love others. We are the living proof that the death of Jesus was not just a vain expression of God's love, but an effective death that achieved the salvation of a people who now love one another sincerely from a pure heart.

Mission must involve not only contact between unbelievers and individual Christians, but between unbelievers and the Christian community. We want to build relationships with unbelievers on their territory, but we also need to introduce them to the network of relationships that makes up the believing community. Indeed people are often attracted to the Christian community before they are attracted to the Christian message. And our approach to mission should involve three elements: (1) building relationships; (2) sharing the gospel message; and (3) including people in community.[20]

The church may never outperform TV shows and music videos, but there is nothing like the community life of the church, nowhere else where diverse people come together in the same way, nowhere else where broken people find a home, nowhere else where grace is experienced and God is present by his Spirit.

I, Tim, think of my own gospel community: a dozen or so people of all ages and backgrounds, eating together on a Thursday night around the table, enjoying simple food yet relishing it as a good gift from God, celebrating together what the Spirit has been doing in our lives, praying for the needs of the world, discussing how we can bless our neighbourhood in Christ's name. There are plenty of other social groups in our neighbourhood. But nowhere else can such diverse individuals come together with a commitment to being family. It is a truly beautiful thing.

3. EVERYDAY PASTORAL CARE

1 Peter 1:22 – 2:3

'Those who dream of [an] idealized community,' warns Dietrich Bonhoeffer, 'demand that it be fulfilled by God, by others, and by themselves. They enter the community of Christians with their demands, set up their own law, and judge one another and even God accordingly.'[1] He continues:

[We] can never live by our own words and deeds, but only by that
one Word and deed that really binds us together, the forgiveness
of sins in Jesus Christ . . . Christian community is not an ideal we
have to realize, but rather a reality created by God in Christ in which
we may participate. The more clearly we learn to recognize that
the ground and strength and promise of all our community is in
Jesus Christ alone, the more calmly we will learn to think about our
community and pray and hope for it.[2]

We've seen that Christians have been born again into a new inheritance that makes us strangers and aliens (1:1–4). We are called to live on the margins. But that act of rebirth also births us into a new family (1:22–23), an alternative community of belonging, a family that is God's demonstration of the gospel. It is the beginning of, and pointer to, the new world which will be our inheritance.

So the gospel community matters. But this does not mean that the gospel Word is less important. Quite the opposite. In 1:22–23, where Peter explicitly links our new birth and our new family, his emphasis is on the means by which we are born anew, i.e. *the enduring Word*: 'For you have been born again, not of perishable seed, but of imperishable, through the living and enduring word of God' (1:23). The Word gives life and continues to give life.

Do not try to 'do' community

What forms and sustains Christian community is, perhaps paradoxically, not a commitment to community per se, but a commitment to the gospel Word. Sometimes people place great emphasis on the importance of community and neglect the gospel Word. Community then becomes a goal to which we work. But Peter says that human activity cannot create life that endures. Indeed an exclusive focus on community will kill it. Only the Word of God can create an enduring community life and love.

Peter calls on us to 'love one another earnestly from a pure heart' (1:22 ESV), a demanding command designed to create a distinctive community. Except that Peter first says that his readers have 'purified [their] souls by [their] obedience to the truth for a sincere brotherly love'. Purified by the gospel for love, we love. The truth purges us of those selfish desires that conflict with love, and this then enables us to love one another earnestly. Love in this way, says Peter, '*for* you have been born again' (1:23).

This is who we are: members of a new family, bound together in brotherly love through the gospel of Jesus and the power of the Spirit. Once again the move is from identity to action. This command is realizable because of who we are in Christ, the new reality that God has produced in our lives through the gospel Word. We get rid of 'all malice and all deceit, hypocrisy, envy, and slander of every kind' (2:1), not through gritted teeth or extra effort. We live a life of love as we crave the spiritual milk of God's enduring Word (2:2). We keep going back to the gospel, believing the gospel, nurturing our hearts with the gospel, tasting the goodness of God in the gospel.

Notice the intensity: 'sincere love', 'love one another deeply', 'from the heart'. It is often said that love is an action, not a feeling. But this is not a biblical idea. Yes, love is an action and a choice. But it is also a feeling, a feeling often produced by making choices, but above all one that arises from our own experience of God's love to us in Christ. Dietrich Bonhoeffer says,

> When God had mercy on us, when God revealed Jesus Christ to us as our brother, when God won our hearts by God's own love, our instruction in Christian love began at the same time. When God was merciful to us, we learned to be merciful with one another. When we received forgiveness instead of judgment, we too were made ready to forgive each other. What God did to us, we then owed to others. The more we received, the more we were able to give; and the more meagre our love for one another, the less we were living by God's mercy and love. Thus God taught us to encounter one another as God has encountered us in Christ. 'Welcome one another, therefore, just as Christ has welcomed you, for the glory of God' (Rom. 15:7).[3]

An enduring community through an enduring Word

Peter's emphasis here is on the enduring nature of the Word of God. Humans are born through the sperm of their father, but this perishable seed creates 'a life that will quickly end' (NLT). However, Christians have been born again through the Word of our new Father and this imperishable Word endures for eternal life.

> For,
>
> 'All men are like grass,
>   and all their glory is like the flowers of the field;
> the grass withers and the flowers fall,
>   but the word of the Lord stands for ever.'
>
> And this is the word that was preached to you.
> (1:24–25)

Human ideas, trends, fashions, accolades are all fleeting. But the Word of the Lord stands for ever.

We need to recognize the link between verses 22 and 23. The latter begins 'for'. Peter intends us to draw a connection between loving one another deeply and being born through the enduring Word of God. Verses 22–23 are about loving one another, 24–25 are about the enduring Word, 2:1 is again about loving one another and 2:2–3 are again about the Word. Because the Word is imperishable, the family is imperishable. We have been born into this family through an imperishable Word, so it is an imperishable family. Human families perish because they break up through conflict or become separated through death. But our new family endures. You will always have Christians to stand by you.

This is precisely what Peter's readers need to hear because they are now 'un-family'. Some will have been rejected by their earthly families. Many will have been rejected by their former friends (4:4). That is why Peter calls on them to love one another sincerely. In the face of worldly rejection, we are to love one another fervently with constancy, commitment and loyalty.

We are to be an alternative family where those who have become 'un-family' can find a home, a place of belonging for displaced exiles. Love these people because they will always be your people. You should not, will not, become 'un-family'. While the word of other people is perishable and their loyalty is fleeting, loyalty in the family of God is lasting because we are bound together by the imperishable Word.

'Crave pure spiritual milk,' says Peter, with all the desperate single-mindedness of newborn babies craving their mother's milk. The Word that gave us life is the Word that continues to give us life. This Word will sustain us, binding us together as we live at the margins.

And craving the milk of God's Word is so much more than acquiring new information. Peter says we are to 'crave pure spiritual milk, so that by it [we] may grow up in [our] salvation, now that [we] have tasted that the Lord is good' (2:2–3). We have acquired a taste for the goodness of God and long to experience that taste again. In 1:23 the perishable is contrasted with the enduring Word of God and in 1:18–19 it is contrasted with the precious blood of Christ. The Word of God is where we discover the precious blood of Christ, where we see the goodness of God in the cross of Jesus.

So we do not read the Bible simply to fill our minds, but to change our hearts, not simply to be *in*formed, but to be *con*formed to the image of Jesus. We read the Bible to stir our affections: our fear, our hope, our love, our desire, our confidence. We read it until our hearts cry out, 'The Lord is good!'

Andy Mason is a church planter in a deprived neighbourhood in London called World's End. He tells the local drug dealers that the Bible is a bit like the crack cocaine they sell because, like illegal drugs, it used to be smuggled into this country. Back in the sixteenth century William Tyndale set about translating the Bible into English. At that time the Bible was only available in Latin and only the clergy had access to it. Tyndale had to work abroad because of the opposition in England, contending with spies, assassins and betrayal. The Bibles he printed had to be smuggled into England. Eventually Tyndale was caught, imprisoned, strangled and burnt. He gave his life so that we could read the Bible in English. His translation formed much of the basis of the King James Version. I, Tim, have a framed page on my wall from a 1551 edition of the Matthew-Tyndale Bible which was the first full English Bible ever printed. It included Tyndale's translation supplemented with a translation by Miles Coverdale of those Bible books which Tyndale had not yet finished.

In the eighteenth century Mary Jones saved for six years to buy a Bible. Mary was the daughter of a poor weaver in Wales. When she became a Christian aged eight, she was desperate to own her own Bible because the nearest copy was at a farmhouse two miles away. So Mary saved up. Then one morning in 1800 when she was fifteen she set out for Bala, walking 25 miles barefoot across the mountains to the home of Thomas Charles. Charles was so moved by her story that he established the British Society to distribute Bibles around the world. The Bible Mary Jones walked 25 miles to buy is now kept in Cambridge University Library.

William Tyndale so craved the pure spiritual milk of God's Word that he spent his life on the run, before dying a martyr's death to bring that milk to the people of England.

Mary Jones so craved the pure spiritual milk of God's Word that as a child she saved up for six years and then walked 25 miles barefoot.

The sense of 1:13 in the original Greek is: 'Set your hope fully on the grace to be given you when Jesus Christ is revealed *by* preparing your minds for action and *by* being self-controlled.' In order to live as God's holy children in a hostile world, we need our hope firmly set on our coming inheritance. We need an eternal perspective that looks beyond our present suffering (1:6). This requires planning. If you go mountaineering you need to be well prepared. You cannot face the hostile environment of a remote mountain in light shoes and without adequate supplies. Similarly, we cannot face the hostile environment of a now-alien culture without preparing our minds for action, filling our minds with the gospel story so that we have confidence in our destination. We sometimes talk of people coping with adversity through great 'internal reserves of strength'. As Christians we need *internal reserves of hope* to live on the margins, and we need to bank deposits of hope through the Word into those internal reserves. We cannot drift into hostility. We will need to be self-controlled.

Preparing our minds for action is literally: 'gird up the loins of [your] mind' (KJV). Imagine a Middle-Eastern man wearing a long robe. He cannot run in a long robe because its folds will flap around his legs. So he gets ready to run by tucking his robe in around his waist. The image almost certainly recalls the Passover night when the people of Israel were to be ready to leave slavery in Egypt. God says, 'This is how you are to eat [the Passover meal]: with your cloak tucked into your belt, your sandals on your feet and your staff in your hand. Eat it in haste; it is the LORD's Passover' (Exodus 12:11). We are like those Israelites. We have been redeemed from an empty, enslaving way of life by the precious blood of Jesus (1:18–19) and now we are heading for our inheritance (1:3–9). We need to be ready for action.

Peter is addressing the family of God's people as a family, calling on them *as a family* to prepare their minds for action. Craving the Word is not a solitary action to be fulfilled primarily alone in a quiet time. This is the Word that creates and sustains family bonds. In contrast to the shifting loyalties and new hostility of former relationships, this is an enduring family created by the enduring Word. The Word also now sustains our new family.

Everyday pastoral care

Let's explore a practical framework for creating Word-centred communities in which people speak this life-sustaining, hope-inspiring, community-building Word to one another. This framework will help equip members of gospel communities to 'speak the truth in love' to one another (Ephesians 4:15).

We begin with five principles of community-based, gospel-centred mutual pastoral care.

1. We pastor one another in everyday life

Think about how teaching and discipleship were done in ancient Israel.

> Hear, O Israel: The LORD our God, the LORD is one. You shall love the LORD your God with all your heart and with all your soul and with all your might. And these words that I command you today shall be on your heart. You shall teach them diligently to your children, and shall talk of them when you sit in your house, and when you walk by the way, and when you lie down, and when you rise.
> (Deuteronomy 6:4–7 ESV)

When you are sitting in your house, when you are walking along the road. Teaching and discipleship were done in the context of ordinary life. When you lie down and when you rise. In other words, not at set times, but throughout your day as opportunities arise.

Think about how Jesus did discipleship and community: around a meal, walking along the road, when reflecting on events.

Or think about Paul. In 1 Thessalonians 2:8 he says, 'We loved you so much that we were delighted to share with you not only the gospel of God but our lives as well, because you had become so dear to us.'

So the context for pastoral care and discipleship is everyday life. Community takes place as we do the chores, watch TV, go to work, eat meals and do a dozen other things. It is about asking someone about their walk with the Lord while you do the dishes together, sharing a car ride to the shops and talking about how the Spirit has spoken to you through God's Word. It is about having people in your home and them seeing how you parent your children. It is about walking the dog together and discovering a pastoral need as you chat. It is about pausing in the supermarket to pray when you learn of a need. It is about having people live with you in your home.

Of course this does not mean anything as crass as saying, 'Come over and watch us parent our children.' Rather, as you share your life, people will see Christian living modelled – or alternatively see Christian grace modelled when you fail to live as you should! We have a generation of young people from dysfunctional homes who need to experience Christian families in action before they themselves become husbands, wives and parents.

So pastoring does not simply equate to intense conversations. Our model is not the therapy session or the hour with a counsellor. We are not doing a slightly different version of that, a model that takes pastoral care out of the ordinary and creates extraordinary interventions. Clearly, there is a place for extraordinary interventions in times of crisis, but relegating pastoral care to the extraordinary creates all sorts of problems.

Consider, for example, the need to admonish or rebuke people. Paul uses a variety of terms to describe the way in which we are to speak the Word into the lives of one another (all emphasis mine):

- Therefore be alert, remembering that for three years I did not cease night or day to *admonish* everyone with tears (Acts 20:31 ESV).
- We urge you, brothers, *admonish* the idle, *encourage* the fainthearted, *help* the weak, be patient with them all (1 Thessalonians 5:14 ESV).
- We proclaim him, *admonishing* and *teaching* everyone with all wisdom, so that we may present everyone perfect in Christ (Colossians 1:28).
- Let the word of Christ dwell in you richly as you *teach* and *admonish* one another with all wisdom (Colossians 3:16).
- I myself am convinced, my brothers, that you yourselves are full of goodness, complete in knowledge and competent to *instruct* [= admonish] one another (Romans 15:14).
- Preach the Word; be prepared in season and out of season; *correct, rebuke* and *encourage* – with great patience and careful instruction (2 Timothy 4:2).
- These, then, are the things you should teach. *Encourage* and *rebuke* with all authority. Do not let anyone despise you (Titus 2:15).

From this list we can discern three key pastoral interventions:

- We teach or instruct where people are ignorant.
- We encourage or comfort where people are fainthearted.
- We rebuke or admonish where people are wayward.

Most of us are comfortable with teaching and encouraging, but we often struggle with rebuking one another.

Or think about the many 'one another' exhortations in the New Testament. Again and again we are told to do certain things to one another within the church: love one another, pray for one another, forgive one another and so on. They are found across all the genres and writers of the New Testament. Together they produce the following main categories:

- Be at peace with one another, forgiving, agreeing, being humble, accepting, forbearing, living in harmony and greeting with a kiss.
- Do not judge, lie or grumble.
- Show hospitality to one another.
- Confess your sins to one another.
- Be kind to one another, concerned, devoted, serving and doing good.
- Instruct and teach one another.
- Admonish, rebuke, exhort and stir up one another.
- Comfort and encourage one another.

Which are *you* personally best at? And which are you worst at? What about your church community? I have done this exercise in many contexts, and universally people say 'rebuke' is the thing they do worst.

This is because we so often take pastoral care out of the context of everyday life and make it something exceptional and extraordinary. If you are rarely rebuked then a rebuke is a big deal. It creates or exacerbates a sense of crisis. Rebuke becomes confrontation. This may be needed in some situations, but often it can be avoided if rebuke has become a normal part of the way we disciple one another.

We are not suggesting it is all about rebuke! Instruction and encouragement are equally important. What we are saying is that everyday pastoral care enables us to have a biblical balance.

Indeed everyday pastoring will often avert the need for confrontation, offering prevention that avoids the need for cure. Hebrews 3:12–13 says, 'See to it, brothers, that none of you has a sinful, unbelieving heart that turns away from the living God. But encourage one another daily, as long as it is called Today, so that none of you may be hardened by sin's deceitfulness.' We are all just a few small steps away from being hardened by sin's deceitfulness. Our hearts are adept at justifying our sinful desires. So we need daily encouragement not to turn away from the living God.

But everyday pastoral care is not the same as spontaneous pastoral care. Do not idolize the spontaneous over the scheduled. People can have rather romantic notions of 'community' as a spontaneous activity in which people hang out without much planning. Somehow community does not count unless it is spontaneous. But there is nothing especially virtuous about spontaneity. When people have busy work lives, community can only happen if people plan to meet together. You may have to plan to do everyday pastoral care. We all have different personalities and different life patterns. Some may need to plan to meet with others or send a regular text or stick a reminder in their schedule. Others will do the hanging out more. We should not value one above the other or assume our way of relating is normative. Let us celebrate diversity within the community.

What we *do* need is 'gospel intentionality'. Ordinary life

with gospel intentionality is all well and good, but if you take out the gospel intentionality then all you have is ordinary life – and everyone does that! We need Christian communities who saturate ordinary life with the gospel. We want 'God-talk' to be normal – talking about what we are reading in the Bible, praying together whenever we share needs, delighting together in the gospel, sharing our spiritual struggles – with both Christians and unbelievers.

2. We pastor one another in community

The primary location for pastoral care is the Christian community. Change is a community project.

The scheduled meetings of the church and the role of a gifted pastor-teacher are clearly important. Our emphasis on ordinary life is not intended to detract from the gifts God has given to his church. But it is important to note the role of more formal teaching times. Paul says, 'It was [Christ] who gave some to be apostles, some to be prophets, some to be evangelists, and some to be pastors and teachers, to prepare God's people for works of service, so that the body of Christ may be built up' (Ephesians 4:11–12). We meet together to be taught by gifted pastor-teachers so that we are equipped to minister to one another and together build up the body of Christ. Pastoral care is not the sole responsibility of pastors any more than evangelism is the sole responsibility of evangelists. The role of pastor-teachers is not to do the pastoring, but to prepare God's people for works of service. Peter calls leaders 'shepherds', but he calls Jesus the 'Chief Shepherd' (5:2, 4). Shepherds in turn need shepherding. They too need a community which points them to 'the Shepherd and Overseer of [their] souls' (2:25).

We need to get away from the idea that a 'minister' in the sense of an ordained church leader does gospel ministry in the pulpit on a Sunday. In a New Testament vision of church the whole community does gospel ministry in the staff room, on the street, in the workplace, at the school gate, in the kitchen. Here in the context of ordinary life they minister to one another and to unbelievers. The church leader is someone who is sacrificed from the frontline (at least in part) to equip everyone else for the frontline. The primary context of mission and community and pastoral care is everyday life.

One reason why change takes place in community is that it is the only context in which pastoral care can take place on an everyday basis. All the other options offer weekly pastoral care at best. Only the shared life of the Christian community offers a context for everyday exhortation and encouragement: 'Encourage one another *daily*, as long as it is called Today, so that none of you may be hardened by sin's deceitfulness' (Hebrews 3:13, my emphasis).

3. We pastor one another over a lifetime

We pastor one another over a lifetime. Sin runs deeply in our hearts. Pastoral issues are complex. Change takes a lifetime and so pastoral care takes a lifetime.

So we cannot expect instant change. We cannot expect to have a conversation with someone that 'sorts them out'. Even if you bring a measure of understanding to a situation, changing the affections of the heart and the habits of behaviour will take time.

It is so important that we remember this – otherwise we will soon be frustrated. 'You just need to believe the gospel' might be technically correct. But we need to recognize that the struggle 'just to believe' is a lifetime struggle. 'Don't be afraid; just believe,' says Jesus to Jairus in Mark 5:36. But the word 'just' does not mean it is easy – especially when faced with the reality of death as Jairus was!

And even when there is resolution, there will still be temptation. Someone may rejoice in God in the face of their depression today. But tomorrow will be a new battle. Someone may come to you in tears because of something their boss said, and you may speak the gospel to their heart and their attitude may change. But next time their boss is unkind, the battle will begin all over again.

It is *everyday* pastoral care that enables this *lifetime* of pastoral care. Because sin is deep-seated we need a daily dose of truth, love, encouragement and exhortation. Because temptation is a daily challenge we need daily to be brought back to the beauties of the gospel.

4. We pastor one another with grace

Here we come to the 'don't-try-this-at-home' qualification. Everyday pastoring sounds great, but please do not try it at home. Unless . . .

In the Sermon on the Mount Jesus says:

> Do not judge, or you too will be judged. For in the same way as you judge others, you will be judged, and with the measure you use, it will be measured to you.
>
> Why do you look at the speck of sawdust in your brother's eye and pay no attention to the plank in your own eye? How can you say to your brother, 'Let me take the speck out of your eye,' when all the time there is a plank in your own eye? You hypocrite, first take the plank out of your own eye, and then you will see clearly to remove the speck from your brother's eye.
>
> (Matthew 7:1–5)

This looks like the counter-text to any notion of everyday pastoral care, which involves some exercise of judgment or discernment. But here we are told not to judge. Or what about removing a speck from your brother's eye when you have a plank in your own? Does this mean we cannot do pastoral care until we have sorted out sin in our own lives? Because if it does, then we will never do it! We have just seen that change is a lifetime task.

The key is the word 'hypocrite': the person who tries to remove the speck is a hypocrite. The hypocrite in the Sermon on the Mount is a self-righteous person who does what he does to be seen by people and establish his own righteousness (6:2, 5, 16). Jesus will soon bring the Sermon to a close with the challenge of two gates, two paths, two foundations. This choice is not so much between a good life and a bad life. When you look over the Sermon, the alternatives are in fact self-reliance and reliance on God, a good life lived for the wrong reasons and a good life that arises from God's grace. The Sermon begins:

> Blessed are the poor in spirit,
>   for theirs is the kingdom of heaven.
> Blessed are those who mourn,
>   for they will be comforted.
> Blessed are the meek,
>   for they will inherit the earth.
> Blessed are those who hunger and thirst for righteousness,
>   for they will be filled.
> (Matthew 5:3–6)

Jesus says, 'Unless your righteousness surpasses that of the Pharisees and the teachers of the law, you will certainly not enter the kingdom of heaven' (5:20). That greater righteousness comes from God to those who hunger for it, to those who are poor in spirit, to the broken, to those who mourn, to those who cry to God for mercy, to those who know themselves to be recipients of God's grace.

So those who should not remove specks from other people's eyes are self-righteous hypocrites. If you do not pastor people out of a strong sense of God's grace, both to you and to them, then you will leave them feeling condemned. And 'there is now no condemnation for those who are in Christ Jesus' (Romans 8:1). If you leave people feeling this way then something has gone horribly wrong in your pastoral care. Self-righteous people make bad pastors. At best they create legalists in their own image; at worst they leave people feeling crushed and condemned.

This means that we should allow people to respond honestly and negatively to our pastoral input. We should always speak as fellow sinners pointing to our Saviour rather than to our way of life or our moral code. We should encourage 360-degree pastoring rather than top-down pastoring. We should be ready for mess and indeed welcome it.

Peter speaks of the cross as an example we should follow (2:21). But there is also something unique about the cross. The heart of Peter's theology is Christ our Substitute, bearing our sins in our place: 'He himself bore our sins in his body on the tree, so that we might die to sins and live for righteousness; by his wounds you have been healed' (2:24; 3:18). The message of grace in the cross must be at the heart of our pastoral work.

Above all, this means that our aim is not to make people moral, but for people to experience joy in Christ. Paul says, 'Convinced of this, I know that I will remain, and I will continue with all of you for your progress and joy in the faith' (Philippians 1:25). The goal of Paul's ministry is joy. This is not some superficial health-and-wealth teaching. It is not about creating a comfortable, complacent life. Indeed Paul experiences joy in the midst of suffering and opposition because his delight is in Christ (Philippians 1:12–21). In Philippians 3:8 he says, 'What is more, I consider everything a loss compared to the surpassing greatness of knowing Christ Jesus my Lord, for whose sake I have lost all things. I consider them rubbish, that I may gain Christ.' Paul's radical commitment to Christ arises from his delight in Christ. And that is the pattern for our pastoral care too. We are not in the business of cajoling people into commitment. Our job is to give people such joy in Christ that the treasures and temptations of this earth look like pathetic alternatives by comparison.

5. We pastor one another with the good news

By 'good news' we mean 'the gospel' – the message of the lordship of Jesus, his saving death on our behalf, eternal life through his resurrection, the welcoming grace of God, the transforming power of the Holy Spirit, the care of a heavenly Father, and so on.

But think of it in terms of 'good news' (which is what the word 'gospel' means). Our pastoral inventions must all offer good news. When we talk with people they need to leave thinking, 'That is such good news. I'm so relieved.' Of course in reality pastoral care is never quite that straightforward. But our goal is to offer good news that brings joy. That is the test of gospel pastoring. Is it good news? Is it gospel good news?

So what else might it be?

First, it might be positive thinking, but not good news. That is the sum of a lot of modern secular counselling: 'You deserve it', 'You can do it', 'Life is not against you.' It is a call to break out of negative thinking. And there is something in this approach. In many ways it is the best the secular world has to offer and often it is effective. But the problem is that sometimes negative thinking is actually right!

I, Tim, am pastoring someone at the moment who is being told by her counsellor that she deserves to get better. Now I sympathize with the intention of the counsellor because this woman suffers from a condition in which people punish themselves. But does she deserve to get better? My friend does not think so. She knows she deserves God's judgment. But I can speak real good news to her: She deserves judgment, but Jesus has taken the judgment she deserves, paid it in full and given her the reward that he deserves so that now she is a child of God. She does not need to punish herself because the punishment was paid in full at the cross. That is good news without any pretending.

So we need to be careful not to offer positive thinking instead of proclaiming good news.

Secondly, it might be good advice, but not good news. It is all too easy, especially with broken people, to give a stream of advice. Maybe you should buy cheaper, non-branded products. Maybe you should spend less time with that person. Maybe you should feed your kids less food with additives.

The problem with this is twofold. First, it distorts your relationship with them. If you are not careful, it puts you into the role of a parent. Or it portrays you as the sorted person and their need is to become like you. Secondly, it is not gospel. At best it might lead to reform. But it will not reconcile them to God, nor change their hearts.

There is a place for advice. It can be an act of love. But we need to spell out for people the nature of what we are saying (especially if we are in a position of authority within the church). We need to distinguish between advice and gospel because they carry very different levels of authority. Advice comes with the authority of my accumulated wisdom, such as it is. The gospel comes with the authority of God and that is a very different proposition.

So we need to be careful not to offer good advice instead of proclaiming good news.

Thirdly, we can proclaim law instead of proclaiming good news. You would think that good evangelical justification-by-faith people would not do this, but we do! The law says, 'You should . . .'; 'You should not sleep with your boyfriend'; 'You should read your Bible every day'; 'You should not get drunk'; 'You should witness to your friends'; 'You should not lose your temper.' Does any of this sound familiar? But that is not good news, not to someone struggling with those issues. It is condemnation.

What the gospel says is this: 'You need not . . .'; 'You need not get drunk because Jesus offers a better refuge'; 'You need not lose your temper because God is in control of the situation.' That is good news!

Sin makes promises. The gospel exposes those promises as false and points to a God who is bigger and better than anything sin offers. That is good news.

Four liberating truths for those we are pastoring

To help pastor our own hearts and to pastor one another let's look at four liberating truths about God. Most of our sinful behaviour and negative emotions arise because we are not believing one of these four truths as we should. That is because behind every sin is a lie about God. In Romans 1:24–25 Paul says,

> Therefore God gave them over in the sinful desires of their hearts to sexual impurity for the degrading of their bodies with one another. They exchanged the truth of God for a lie, and worshipped and served created things rather than the Creator – who is for ever praised. Amen.

We exchange the truth about God for a lie. And because we do not believe in God as we should, something else comes to matter more to us than God. Sin is always the result of misplaced affections. Sin makes promises. When we believe those promises, we think sin offers more than God. This lie warps our affections. Our love, our delight, our fear, our hope become misplaced.

This does not necessarily mean that we are heretics or untaught. We are not talking about confessional belief, but functional belief. Most of our problems arise not because we need new truth that we do not yet have (though sometimes this is the case), but because we need truths we already know pushed down into the everyday realities of our lives. We need to feel in our hearts the truth we already know in our heads.

So our role as those committed to pastoring one another is to speak the truth to one another in the everyday realities of one another's lives. If we can identify the lie behind the sin then we can speak the truth more effectively. This is the truth that will, as Jesus promised, set us free. We need to ask ourselves: What is the lie and what is the corresponding gospel promise? What is being substituted for Jesus and what is the corresponding truth about Jesus that offers hope? The following four liberating truths about God (the 'four Gs') target nearly all our sinful behaviour and negative emotions.[4]

1. God is great – so we do not have to be in control
We often want to be in control so we dominate people or manipulate them. Or we fear things being out of control so we worry or overwork. But God is sovereign. He is in control. Things may not always go the way we want, but God uses everything that happens to us for our good.

2. God is glorious – so we do not have to fear others

We often sin because we crave the approval of other people or fear their rejection. The Bible calls this 'the fear of man'. We live to please other people or we are controlled by peer pressure. The Bible's answer is the fear of God. God is the glorious One whom we should fear, the One whose approval matters most and the One whose approval we have in Jesus Christ.

3. God is good – so we do not have to look elsewhere

Sin often leads to pleasure, but this is empty and temporary. Only God brings true and lasting joy. The pleasures of sin are quick and immediate, so we need faith to turn to God for lasting joy.

4. God is gracious – so we do not have to prove ourselves

Many people act out of a desire to prove themselves. On the surface they may look impressive because they achieve many things or live good lives. When things go well they are proud, but when things go bad they are crushed. They may look down on others because this makes them feel better about themselves, or become bitter when their hard work is not rewarded in the way they expect. It is also this desire that makes us determined to win an argument. The good news is that, while we can never justify ourselves before God, God has justified us through Jesus Christ. Jesus has done it all, so we have nothing left to prove.

Suppose someone is angry.

They might be angry because they do not believe that **God is great** or that he is in control. They may believe in the providence of God in theory but in practice they are not trusting God to provide for their needs. They feel the need to be in control and when life is not under their control (as it will not be sooner or later) they get angry.

Or they may be angry because they do not believe that **God is glorious**. Of course on Sunday they sing that he is robed in majesty. But on Monday morning their boss is the one they fear. Their boss looms large in their mind, eclipsing God. They are desperate for his approval, so when they have a bad day or a colleague lets them down they become angry. Their anger is an expression of their fear. The biblical answer is not to try to fear their boss less but to fear God more: to see God in his glory, majesty, holiness, love and beauty so that he totally eclipses their boss. That is the word we need to speak to them.

Or they may be angry because they do not believe that **God is good**. They are not looking to God for satisfaction and so they look elsewhere: to their work, their leisure, their family, their possessions, their girlfriend or the girlfriend they wish they had. And if any of those things are threatened then they become angry.

Or they may be angry because they do not believe **God is gracious**. Maybe they have a contractual view of their relationship with God. They think that if they live an obedient life then God will bless them. They give up things for God and think God owes them something in return. They may even have a particular blessing in mind. They may long for a husband and think God will provide one if they live a good life. When God does not provide him, they become embittered. They may not articulate that anger as anger against God. It may be an ill-defined resentment or they may lash out randomly at other people. But underneath it all is an anger against God. They need to rediscover the grace of God, for God does not treat us on a contractual basis. Or rather he does, but that contract is the new covenant under which he forgives our sins on the basis of the blood of his Son. We do not get what we deserve because what we deserve is hell. What we get instead is God himself.

Speaking these truths does not mean simply saying something like, 'You just need to fear God more.' These truths are not to be wielded like accusations along the lines of: 'Your problem is that you don't believe God is great.' That is not good news. Instead we are called to portray God to one another in all his glory and beauty and majesty, singing songs and telling stories that speak of his glory, and then making the connections to everyday life. It means presenting the truth in a way that captures the imagination. The framework of these four liberating truths is just a diagnostic toolkit. Do not be satisfied with repeating the bald statements that God is great, glorious, good and gracious. Draw upon all your knowledge of the Bible story, all the texts you have memorized, all the hymns and songs you know to express these truths with real colour and texture.

Notice too how a symptom (in this case anger) does not automatically equate to one specific truth. People are complicated. What is more, they have all sorts of issues going on in their hearts at the same time. And the heart is deceitful above all things. We will need to explore people's presenting issues to discern underlying causes.

Misplaced affections are rarely revealed on Sunday mornings when people are on their best behaviour. That is why sharing life in the context of everyday life is so vital. This is when our hearts are revealed, when we face the pressures of life or in our interaction with other people with whom we find it hard to live.

But there is comforting news. Speaking the truth about God will do no harm. You may not be able to identify precisely what is going on in a person's heart. If they need to hear that God is gracious and you remind them that God is great then you may not get it right, but you will not get it wrong! No-one will ever be damaged by being reminded that God is their heavenly Father.

What is more, while we may not be able to discern the inner workings of a person's heart, God's Word does its own analysis:

> For the word of God is living and active. Sharper than any
> double-edged sword, it penetrates even to dividing soul and spirit,
> joints and marrow; it judges the thoughts and attitudes of the heart.
> Nothing in all creation is hidden from God's sight. Everything is
> uncovered and laid bare before the eyes of him to whom we must
> give account.
>
> (Hebrews 4:12–13)

The Spirit of God is 'the Paraclete' or 'the Counsellor'. When we speak the Spirit-inspired Word of God, the Spirit uses that Word to search and counsel the heart.

> The law of the LORD is perfect,
>   reviving the soul.
> The statutes of the LORD are trustworthy,
>   making wise the simple.
>
> (Psalm 19:7)

Four liberating truths for those who pastor

These four truths are great truths to apply to those we are pastoring. But it is important also to apply them to ourselves *as pastors*. For the most part, our pastoral interventions go wrong not because we lack technique or knowledge or experience but because *we as pastors* have failed truly to believe one of these four truths about God. To state the obvious, there are two sinners involved in any pastoral relationship!

So let's consider the implications of not believing these four truths for us as we pastor others.

1. God is great – so we do not have to be in control

Effects of a faithless response on our ability to pastor.
We will be over-controlling, the arbiter of truth. We want
immediately to correct every error for fear people might
go astray or that we might lose control, so we do not give
people time to grow. When we speak truth to people's lives
we will be intense and overbearing because we want to solve
the problem. We fear what might happen to this person so
we talk at them, not to them. We do not give them space to
change or to disagree.

Or we may become risk-averse. We will not take risks
with people or situations because we fear that things will go
wrong. We may be indecisive because we fear making the
wrong choice. We may slip into a form of clericalism in which
we will not trust others to do God's work because we fear
they might do it wrong, or we may micro-manage situations.

Effects of faithful response. Our pastoral care will be
relaxed and patient. We will give people space to change and
time to grow. When we talk with individuals, we will not feel
the need to sort everything out in one go. We will give them a
chance to talk and space to disagree. At the same time we will
be able to take risks because we trust the outcome to God's
sovereign care. We will give away power and responsibility
because we do not think that everything depends on us.

2. God is glorious – so we do not have to fear others

Effects of a faithless response on our ability to pastor. If
not trusting the greatness of God leads to over-pastoring then
not fearing our glorious God will lead to under-pastoring.
If we fear people more than we fear God then we may be
reluctant to speak the truth. We will not confront people
because we are worried that they might dislike or reject us. We
may avoid difficult decisions that might upset people. Or we

may second-guess what people are thinking because we are trying to anticipate what will please them. You can sometimes discern this in discussions when a fearful person routinely glances at a particular person to gauge his or her reaction.

Or we may treat sin not in relation to a holy God, but in terms of what others think of it. In other words, respectability will matter more than holiness. We will treat 'unrespectable' sins more seriously than other sins because we are driven by people's opinions.

Another potential symptom is that we will gravitate towards activities that are 'up front' because our goal in ministry is to be admired. We become 'slaves to praise'. Or there is a gap between our public and private persona. The holiness that matters to us is public holiness.

Effects of faithful response. If, however, we believe that God is glorious and that he is to be feared then we will not be controlled by other people. Only then, in fact, will we be truly free to serve them in love. When you are controlled by the opinions of others your actions are self-serving. Their aim is a good reputation. Only when the glory of God sets you free from the 'fear of man' are you free to serve others in love. Then you are free to speak the truth people need to hear, not what they want to hear. And we ourselves can also be vulnerable before others, rejoicing in God's vindication or justification.

3. God is good – so we do not have to look elsewhere
Effects of a faithless response on our ability to pastor. If we do not believe that God is good and the one who truly satisfies, then we may be reluctant to serve, we may do the minimum, serve begrudgingly or with a sense of compulsion, viewing ministry as a burden. People might find us unapproachable because they pick up signals that we do not want

to be bothered. Or we may look for satisfaction in other things or not stick at tasks we dislike. We will not do the hard work of pastoral care, hanging out with people we are not naturally attracted to or challenging people's behaviour. We will avoid difficult conversations and messy people. Instead we will only be interested in doing what is fun.

Effects of faithful response. If, however, we are finding joy in God then we will serve with passion and enthusiasm. We will be characterized by generosity, simplicity and energy. Our lives will be winsome and welcoming.

4. God is gracious – so we do not have to prove ourselves

Effects of a faithless response on our ability to pastor. We may find our identity in ministry rather than in Christ and so overwork or make others feel guilty through our high expectations. Or we may envy others whose ministry is more successful, or take pride in our success. We ourselves will take criticism badly, being defensive or defeated, because our identity is tied up in our achievements and not in Christ's achievements on our behalf. There is a danger that our lives can become so busy and stressed because we are trying to prove ourselves that we fail to model good news to people.

We will be functional legalists who think that behaviour matters more than motives, who want to avoid mess in favour of respectability, and condemn those who do not measure up. We will impose a set of expectations on other people that wears them down under the weight of joyless duty. If we do not believe that God is gracious then we will not want our sins to be exposed, so we may not ask people hard questions about their spiritual life for fear of being asked them in return.

Effects of faithful response. If we rest on the grace of God and find our identity in Christ then our lives and ministry will characterized by peace and rest, joy and freedom, confidence and humility, compassion and kindness. We will not rejoice when others fail. Our concern will be to bless rather than impress. We will not need the affirmation of other people and we will be free from the need to defend ourselves. There will be a transparency and vulnerability about our lives because we will not feel the need to hide our sin. So we will create a context in which other people feel able to share their struggles.

Use the following table to examine your own pastoral care.

Is your pastoral care shaped by confidence in the four Gs?	Contrary indicators
God is great – so we do not have to be in control	• you are overbearing • you are inflexible or risk-averse • you are impatient with people • you avoid responsibility
God is glorious – so we do not have to fear others	• you avoid confrontation • you crave approval • you behave differently around certain people • you pretend or hide your true self
God is good – so we do not have to look elsewhere	• you feel ministry is a burden • you often complain • you make people feel a burden of duty • you don't stick at things
God is gracious – so we do not have to prove ourselves	• you take criticism and failure badly • you find it hard to relax • you are proud or envy the success of others • you make people feel guilty

Most poor pastoral care comes down to either over-pastoring or under-pastoring. *Over-pastoring* is a tendency to dominate or manipulate or a tendency to be overbearing and overly intense when we speak. *Under-pastoring* is a failure to challenge when we should or to avoid difficult people and difficult conversations. A failure to believe that:

- God is great leads to over-pastoring. (We think people need us to save them.)
- God is glorious leads to under-pastoring. (We fear how people will respond to us.)
- God is good leads to under-pastoring. (We avoid difficult situations.)
- God is gracious lead to over-pastoring. (We try to prove ourselves by sorting people.)

Do you see yourself in any of the descriptions of pastors above? Do you have a tendency to over-pastor or under-pastor? The point is not merely to correct our behaviour ('I tend to over-pastor so I need to restrain myself more'). No, the point is to see, believe, embrace, delight in the truth about God. If you over-pastor because you do not trust God's sovereign care then focus particularly on God's sovereign care. Meditate on your heavenly Father, on his care of creation, on the gift of his Son, on the mysterious sovereignty of the cross. Invite others to challenge you to trust his sovereignty and speak to you often of his greatness. Then the truth will set you free to be a good pastor.

4. EVERYDAY MISSION

1 Peter 2:9 – 3:16

The church is the people of God called to display the goodness of his reign to the world, the bride of Christ formed
through his reconciling death. It is the community of grace
united by the empowering presence of the Holy Spirit.
Church is not so much about how we structure ourselves,
where we meet, how often we meet, nor even what we do
whenever we meet. Church is about who we are as the people
of God, living distinctively by grace through the Spirit under
the reign of King Jesus, to the glory of our heavenly Father.
These are the elements that should preoccupy us. Everything
else then becomes a way of presenting, harnessing and pro-
tecting this.

Reverse engineering is the process of dismantling an object
to see what it is for and how it works. If we reverse engineer

John's vision of the new Jerusalem at the climax of the Bible story, this allows us to see what the whole Bible story is for and how it works. Noting the way John's vision of the new creation becomes a vision of a garden-city in the shape of a temple, Greg Beale says, 'The new creation and Jerusalem are none other than God's tabernacle . . . the true temple of God's special presence.'[7] Revelation 21:3 says literally, 'Behold, the tabernacle of God is among men and he will dwell among them.' Paul Barnett comments: 'Here is an astonishing teaching. The New Heaven and New Earth is the New Jerusalem, which is the Bride of Christ, both of which depict the gathered community of the redeemed ones. The new creation is the church, the church of the end time.'[8] In Revelation 22 'the river of the water of life' flows from 'the throne of God and of the Lamb' (22:1). The word John uses to describes the tree that brings healing to the nations is not the normal word for tree, but a word that refers to timber and is used in the New Testament to refer to the cross (Acts 5:30; 10:39; 13:29; Galatians 3:13; 1 Peter 2:24). It is the glory of the sacrificed Lamb which illuminates the new creation (Revelation 21:23). So central to this climactic vision is the Redeemer and his redeemed people. This is the fulfilment of God's eternal plan 'to bring all things in heaven and on earth together under one head, even Christ' (Ephesians 1:10). This is where the story is going. In the meantime, 'God placed all things under his feet and appointed him to be head over everything for the church, which is his body, the fulness of him who fills everything in every way' (Ephesians 1:22–23). God's ultimate purpose is not to see a solitary king ruling over ad hoc individuals, but a king with his people. Eternity is filled with the church.

Understanding the Bible story in this way, it is easy to see why church planting is so important. The church is God's primary mission strategy in the world. Our strategy therefore must be to litter the world with communities of light. All of this encapsulates God's eternal purpose, at the heart of which are Christ and his people.

Everyday mission

One of the central themes of this book is that our marginal status as Christians in the West requires us to think differently about mission. One way to do this is by dropping our preoccupation with 'church'.

If words are defined by usage rather than etymology, then the contemporary usage of 'church' means that we are almost certainly miscommunicating when we use it. We learn from an early age that 'church' is a building. Or we see it as an institution, a relic of a bygone age, an organization in terminal decline. Nick Spencer and Graham Tomlin claim: 'The most important social fact about the church is that it is an institution, and institutions are deeply unpopular in modern Britain.'[1] And it does not help that many Christians function as if church were a meeting, an event which we attend and to which we invite people. Or we think of it as an entity with structures and formalities, such as constitutions, ministers, elders and committees.

If anything is a hindrance to people being introduced to Jesus then it has to be disposable. Yes, the cross offends. Christ crucified will always be a stumbling block. But we must remove every other offence. We must do all we can to live in a way that exposes and manifests the true nature of the cross.

So this is a plea, not necessarily to ditch the word 'church' (though William Tyndale replaced it with 'congregation' in his translation of the Bible into English), but for us to be preoccupied with being truly that which the term designates. This is not some misguided interest in rediscovering the purity of a New Testament model, as if the New Testament presents one definitive blueprint. Instead, it arises from a passion for others to discover the grace that comes to us in Christ.

Peter says,

> You are a chosen people, a royal priesthood, a holy nation, a people belonging to God, that you may declare the praises of him who called you out of darkness into his wonderful light. Once you were not a people, but now you are the people of God; once you had not received mercy, but now you have received mercy.
> (2:9–10)

He describes the church, using a litany of Old Testament allusions, particularly to Exodus 19:4–6, Isaiah 43:20–21 and Hosea 2:23.

1 Peter 2:9–10	*Main Old Testament allusions*
You are a chosen people	my chosen people (Isaiah 43:20 ESV)
a royal priesthood	a kingdom of priests (Exodus 19:6)
a holy nation	a holy nation (Exodus 19:6)
a people belonging to God	my treasured possession (Exodus 19:5); my people (Isaiah 43:20)
that you may declare the praises of him who called you . . .	that they might declare my praise (Isaiah 43:21 ESV)
Once you were not a people, but now you are the people of God	I will say to Not My People, 'You are my people' (Hosea 2:23 ESV)

once you had not received mercy, but now you have received mercy	I will have mercy on No Mercy (Hosea 2:23 ESV)

Old Testament citations in the New Testament are like hypertext links. You click on them to discover more than first meets the eye. They are not random similarities, but usually indicate substantive theological background material. Verses 9–10 are no exception.

Let's rewind to the Old Testament. Exodus 19:4–6 contains the words God spoke to Israel at Sinai to introduce the Mosaic covenant. As he is about to give God's people the Ten Commandments, Moses tells them how they should see themselves and outlines the purpose of the covenant. Israel is called to be a priestly kingdom. Ordinarily priests made God known to the people and offered sacrifices. Now the whole of Israel as a community is to be priestly: making God known to the nations and calling the nations to find atonement through sacrifice. Peter's reference to a royal priesthood is more than an affirmation of the Reformation doctrine of the priesthood of believers (though in the light of 2:5 it is certainly not less than this). Peter is talking about our corporate identity as God's priestly people whose life together commends the goodness of his kingdom. Similarly, God's people are to be a holy or distinct nation, just as God himself is holy. God is carving out one place on earth where the goodness and freedom of his kingdom can be seen. In other words, as we've seen already, the community of God's people is to be a missional community. The law is missional in intent, defining the distinctive community life that will draw the nations to God.

The same missional ideas are present in Isaiah 43, as Isaiah looks ahead to the exile of God's people in Babylon, an exile in which Peter sees his readers (1:1; 5:13). Exile was the curse that Moses warned would fall if Israel failed to be a light to the nations through her faithfulness to the covenant (Deuteronomy 28:49–68). But Isaiah says that God is going to lead them home through a new exodus. The One who brought his people through the Red Sea, led them through the desert and gave them water to drink is 'doing a new thing' (Isaiah 43:16–20). Peter has already described the death of Jesus as a new Passover (1:18–19). Now God's redeemed people are again to declare his praises.

This calling on God's people to attract the world to God through the quality of our lives is precisely how Peter goes on to apply his allusions to the Old Testament:

> Dear friends, I urge you, as aliens and strangers in the world, to abstain from sinful desires, which war against your soul. Live such good lives among the pagans that, though they accuse you of doing wrong, they may see your good deeds and glorify God on the day he visits us.
>
> (2:11–12)

The word 'church' is first used of God's people when they are gathered at Mount Sinai. The Greek version of the Old Testament uses the word *ekklēsia* in Deuteronomy 9:10 and 10:4, and Stephen uses *ekklēsia* to describe Israel at Sinai in Acts 7:38. Gathered around Mount Sinai, the church is told to live in such a way that it will commend God to the nations. In 1 Peter 2:9–12 Peter again brings us to Mount Sinai and again we are called to commend God to the nations through our lives.

Peter also seems to have in mind the words of Jesus when he was talking to his newly formed messianic community (Matthew 5:14–16). Our community life gives both substance and credence to our words. It is the means by which our commendation of God's glory and grace is vindicated. We are to live in the midst of an antagonistic world so that others will ask the reason for our hope (3:15).

This is the mission strategy Peter gives to marginalized congregations living in a hostile context. Respond to hostility with good deeds. Live such good lives that people glorify God.

Of course good works on their own are not sufficient. Proclamation matters. We are called to 'declare' God's praises (2:9). We are to be ready to give 'an answer to everyone who asks [us] to give the reason for the hope that [we] have' (3:15). The gospel is a Word. But the primary context in which that Word is proclaimed is the everyday life of the Christian community.

Verses 11–12 are just the headline. Peter then goes on to apply this mission strategy to our life in society (2:13–17), in the workplace (2:18–25) and in the home (3:1–7). In each case Peter addresses those who face hostility because they follow Christ. The person who receives 'unjust suffering because he is conscious of God' is a reference to someone suffering as a Christian' (2:19).[2] Again, while Peter's words apply to the witness of all wives, his focus is on those whose husbands 'do not believe the word' (3:1). In each case we are called to good works (2:15, 20; 3:1–2), to show submission and have respect for others (2:13, 17, 18; 3:1–2). Peter also repeats his reminder that our fear of God liberates us to serve others in the face of hostility (2:17; 3:6). Centrally, there is a repeated expectation that, echoing 2:12, our good works will have a missional impact. 'For it is God's will that by doing good you should silence the ignorant talk of foolish men' (2:15). 'They may be won over without words by the behaviour of their wives' (3:1). Interestingly, although we may think the husband's traditionally more dominant role might mean unbelieving wives are more likely to be converted through their believing husbands, research by John Finney has found that unbelieving husbands are more likely to be converted by believing wives, which would appear to bear out the hope of 1 Peter 3:1–2.[3]

And it is not simply that 'ordinary' Christians live good lives that enable them to invite friends to 'evangelistic events'. Our lives *are* the evangelistic events. Our life together is the apologetic. Let us affirm and celebrate ordinary Christians living ordinary life in Christ's name. This is the frontline of mission. Mark Greene says,

> The vast majority of Christians feel that they do not get any significant support for their daily work from the teaching, preaching, prayer, worship, pastoral, group aspect of local church life. No support for how they spend 50 percent of their waking lives. As one teacher put it: 'I spend an hour a week teaching Sunday school and they haul my up to the front of the church to pray for me. The rest of the week I'm a full-time teacher and the church has never prayed for me. That says it all.'[4]

When we think of evangelism we should not first think of guest services, evangelistic courses, street preaching or door knocking. We should think of Gary at a meeting of the residents' association, Hannah in her office, Sharon serving a meal to her husband.

Here is an exercise to help identify opportunities for everyday mission.[5] Think of all the activities, however mundane, that make up your normal (1) *daily routine* (like travelling to work, eating meals, chores, walking the dog, playing with the children); (2) *weekly routine* (like grocery shopping, watching favourite television programmes, getting exercise);

and (3) *monthly routine* (like gardening, getting a haircut, going to the cinema). You should have a long list. For each one, ask whether you could add: (1) *a community component* by involving another member of your Christian community; (2) *a missional component* by involving an unbeliever; and (3) *a gospel component* by identifying opportunities to talk about Jesus.

Clearly not everything you do can be done with someone else. But this exercise reveals just how many opportunities we do have. You might knock on a friend's door as you walk the dog to see if they want to walk with you. You might offer an elderly neighbour a ride when you drive to the supermarket. You might meet a member of the Christian community for breakfast one morning a week or agree to ride on the same bus to work. Instead of reading your Christian book in the canteen, you might take the opportunity to get to know your colleagues. None of this is adding anything to your schedule, for these are all activities in which you are already engaged. One of the things people in my gospel community do, for example, is watch certain television programmes together, programmes such as *The Apprentice* or *Britain's Got Talent* that are in any case best watched with a group commentary. They get together, inviting Christians and non-Christians to watch with them. You are going to be watching it anyway so why not watch with other people, share the experience and see what opportunities this presents?

Leave the house in the evenings. Sounds simple? Yet you know how it is, especially in winter. It has been a tiring day at work and now it's dark. The easiest thing is to slump in the front of the television or surf the internet or play on the Xbox. Get out! It does not matter where you go as long as you go with gospel intentionality. Walk out through the door and then decide what to do! Drop round to the home of another member of your missional community. Pop round to a friend. Take a cake to a neighbour. Attend a local community group. Go to the cinema. Hang out in a café. Go for a walk with a friend.

Jonathan Dodson from Austen City Life in Texas suggests eight easy ways to be missional.[6] 'Missional,' he comments, 'is not an event we tack onto our already busy lives. It is our life. Mission should be the way we live, not something we add onto life . . . We can be missional in everyday ways without even overloading our schedules. Here are a few suggestions.' (We suggest that you adapt these to suit your culture.)

1. **Eat with non-Christians**. We all eat three meals a day. Why not make a habit of sharing one of those meals with a non-Christian or with a family of non-Christians? Go to lunch with a co-worker, not by yourself. Invite the neighbours over for family dinner. If it's too much work to cook a big dinner, just order pizza and put the focus on conversation. When you go out for a meal, invite others. Or take your family to family-style restaurants where you can sit at a table with strangers and strike up a conversation. Cook out and invite Christians and non-Christians. *Flee the Christian subculture.*

2. **Walk, don't drive**. If you live in a walkable area, make a practice of getting out and walking around your neighbourhood, apartment complex or campus. Instead of driving to the mailbox, convenience store, or apartment office, walk to get mail, groceries and stuff. Be deliberate in your walk. Say hello to people you don't know. Strike up conversations. Attract attention by walking the dog or bringing the kids. Make friends. Get out of your house! Take an interest in your neighbours. Ask questions. Pray as you go. *Save some gas, the planet, and some people.*

3. **Be a regular**. Instead of hopping all over the city for gas, groceries, haircuts, eating out and coffee, go to the same places. Get to know the staff. Go to the same places at the

same times. Smile. Ask questions. Be a regular. I have friends at coffee shops all over the city. My friends at Starbucks donate a ton of leftover pastries to our church two to three times a week. We use them for church gatherings and occasionally give them to the homeless. Build relationships. *Be a regular.*

4. **Hobby with non-Christians**. Pick a hobby that you can share. Get out and do something you enjoy with others. Try City League sports. Local rowing and cycling teams. Share your hobby by teaching lessons. Teach sewing lessons, piano lessons, violin, guitar, knitting, tennis lessons. Be prayerful. Be intentional. Be winsome. Have fun. *Be yourself.*

5. **Talk to your co-workers.** How hard is that? Take your breaks with intentionality. Go out with your team or task force after work. Show interest in your co-workers. Pick four and pray for them. Form mums and toddlers groups in your neighbourhood and don't make them exclusively Christian. Schedule play dates with the neighbours' kids. *Work on mission.*

6. **Volunteer with non-profits.** Find a non-profit organization in your part of the city and take a Saturday a month to serve your city. Bring your neighbours, your friends, or your small group. Spend time with your church serving your city. Once a month. *You can do it!*

7. **Participate in city events**. Instead of playing Xbox, watching TV or surfing the net, participate in city events. Go to fundraisers, festivals, clean-ups, summer shows and concerts. Participate missionally. Strike up conversation. Study the culture. Reflect on what you see and hear. Pray for the city. Love the city. *Participate with the city.*

8. **Serve your neighbours.** Help a neighbour by weeding, mowing, building a cabinet, fixing a car. Stop by the neighbourhood association or apartment office and ask if there is anything you can do to help improve things. Ask your local

police and fire stations if there is anything you can do to help them. Get creative. *Just serve!*

Love Jesus, love people, love life

So everyday mission is not a technique or a programme. You cannot programme an unprogrammed church! We cannot offer you five steps to get your church doing everyday mission. The core elements are loving Jesus, loving people, loving life.

Love Jesus. Enthusiasm for evangelism doesn't begin with evangelism at all. Exhortations to evangelize just leave us feeling useless. Driven by guilt, we try 'turning' the conversation at work round to spiritual things with horrible, crunching gear changes or we knock on a few doors to little effect. And so we give up. Again. And feel guilty. Again.

Love and passion and enthusiasm are infectious. We see that everywhere. If you are doing something – playing a game, watching a film, walking in the country – and someone says, 'This is really boring', the whole atmosphere goes flat. But if someone is excited about it then other people get excited. You will never attract people to Jesus if you are not excited about Jesus yourself. Enthusiasm creates interest. Passions breeds passion.

Loving Jesus is also the antidote to legalism. If I give you rules and expectations then your faith will quickly become a formal, routine duty and that will sap your energy. The joy of the Lord is our strength, says Nehemiah (8:10), but there is no joy in obeying rules. Enthusiasm for evangelism begins with an enthusiasm for Jesus. My willingness to speak of Jesus arises from my delight in Jesus. And loving Jesus also counters perhaps our main impediment to evangelism which is what the Bible calls 'the fear of man' – our desire for approval and our fear of rejection. A passion for Jesus means that he matters more to us than other people. His opinion is the one that counts.

Loving Jesus is not a technique. Do not even think about how you can communicate a passion for Jesus to others. Be passionate about him. Meditate on him until he captures your heart afresh.

Love people. If the first element in evangelism is being passionate about Jesus, then the second is being passionate about people: not just seeing them as evangelistic fodder or targets for gospel salvos, but as people to love. Love will care for all their needs – physical, social, emotional. But gospel love also recognizes our greatest need which is to know God through Christ. So true love will always want to introduce people to our greatest friend, Jesus.

And as with loving Jesus, loving people is not a technique. We sometimes meet people who are excited about mission and community, but they do not love people. They love the *idea* of community, but they do not love the real people that make up that community. They love discussing missiology but they do not love the real people whom we encounter in mission. If you do not feel a love for people then pray that God will melt your heart and give you a love for specific people.

Love life. Thirdly, we need to be people who love life. Christians should be the world's natural enthusiasts. We see the world as a theatre of God's glory. OK, we know it is marred by sin and scarred by suffering, but we also see in it many good things from God. We know that 'everything God created is good, and nothing is to be rejected if it is received with thanksgiving' (1 Timothy 4:4). Sport, gardening, technology, literature, DIY, work, cars, food, fashion – all these things are good gifts from God for our enjoyment. Our job is to have fun to the glory of God! Gardening may never become a major leisure activity for you, but when you meet a keen gardener, you should be interested, enthusiastic, excited by this person's joy in God's good world.

This attitude of enthusiasm reflects a robust doctrine of creation. But it is also a great way of connecting with people. Bill is an American friend of mine. He does not really get football (soccer), rugby or cricket. But when he watches a game with us he is enthusiastic. He gets pleasure from our pleasure. It's the same with a hundred and one other topics. If Bill finds out that you are interested in something then the next time you meet you will find he has done some research. It is not a technique. It is not faked. He has a godly curiosity and delight in everything. And funnily enough, people love having Bill around.

Everyday missionaries

Jez moved to a new city a few months ago with a vision to plant a church. His time has been filled with speaking to churches, raising funds, designing a website, producing a vision video. Our instinct tells us that he will be a success. A couple of years down the line people will be asking him to speak on church planting because he will be seen as a 'successful' church planter. When he launches the church, he will have musicians, sound equipment, a great venue – the full works. Jez is a good man with ability, character and charisma. And what he is doing is great.

But the problem is that there are not many people around with his abilities or resources or charisma. Jez is playing to his strengths and he is using his God-given gifting. But if that is what church planting requires, then quite honestly we are not going to see many churches planted.

It is the same with the prevailing model of church planting. This involves a large church sending a group of thirty to fifty people, led by a fully supported minister. It is exciting when this happens. But if that is what church planting requires then we are not going to see many churches planted.

The problem is that Jez's approach to church is beyond most Christians. At best they fill rotas; at worst they are passive observers. Church becomes a performance in which most people are observers of the super-talented. The people of God are disenfranchised.

One of our ambitions is to take the idea of gospel ministry as the primary preserve of the professionals and 'give it back' to the masses. Christianity has always been a populist movement. Stuart Murray says,

> We know of few 'missionaries' in pre-Christendom. Mission depended primarily on the witness of unknown Christians – countless acts of kindness, family and friendship connections, provocative discipleship and significant conversations. Evangelism was a lifestyle, not a specialist activity.[9]

One of the key benefits of everyday mission is that it enfranchises each and every one of us. Everyday mission requires everyday missionaries rather than superheroes of the faith. We need to recapture the sense that gospel ministry is not something done by pastors with the support of ordinary Christians, but something done by ordinary Christians with the support of pastors.

Stealth church

In our culture Christianity is a bit like a bad dream, the details of which you cannot quite remember, but which has left you with a sense of unease that you want to be rid of. So we need to think about doing *church under the radar*. People are alert to religion in general and Christianity in particular. It is on their radar. They regard it as a threat, an intruder, something invasive that they want to avoid. So instead of 'opening a church' when we plant, perhaps we need to concentrate more on being a group of disciples who take following Christ seriously. The term 'Christianity' occurs zero times in the Bible. The term 'Christian' occurs no more than three times. But the term 'disciple' is found over 260 times.

A lot of people follow what might be called 'the Kinsella approach' to church planting. In the film *Field of Dreams* a farmer called Ray Kinsella (played by Kevin Costner) has a dream in which he is told to build a baseball diamond on his farm in an out-of-the-way part of Iowa. It is a crazy idea but he becomes persuaded that he has to do it. Somehow it will be the making of his farm and save him from foreclosure. He clings to the belief that people will turn up to watch baseball – and pay for the privilege. In one conversation Terrance Mann, a reclusive author, says,

> Ray, people will come. They'll come to Iowa for reasons they can't even fathom. They'll turn up your driveway not knowing for sure why they're doing it . . . They'll pass over the money without even thinking about it: for it is money they have and peace they lack . . . The memories will be so thick they'll have to brush them away from their faces. People will come, Ray. The one constant through all the years, Ray, has been baseball. America has rolled by like an army of steamrollers. It has been erased like a blackboard, rebuilt and erased again. But baseball has marked the time . . . People will come, Ray. People will most definitely come.

We naively think that Christianity is like baseball: 'the one constant through all the years'. So all we need to do is open a building or run a meeting and 'the people will come, the people will most definitely come!' But, as we've seen already, the *vast* majority are stubbornly staying away.

We cannot equate church with its meetings. The New Testament word we translate as 'church' is *ekklēsia* or 'gathering'. It was the common term for any gathering, including political meetings (Acts 19:39) or even a riotous mob (Acts 19:32). This background causes some to argue in a reductionistic way that 'church' only exists in the event of a gathering. But this makes passages like Acts 9:31 difficult to understand: 'Then the church throughout Judea, Galilee and Samaria enjoyed a time of peace. It was strengthened; and encouraged by the Holy Spirit, it grew in numbers, living in the fear of the Lord.' Here the term 'church' in the singular is used to refer to what would have been multiple 'churches' throughout a region of 5,000 square miles.

So the New Testament usage suggests a more developed application. It refers to 'those whom the Lord has gathered to himself' rather than simply 'those who gather'. Paul is not merely talking about an act of gathering, for example, when he writes to Timothy about the appointment of elders. He draws a direct connection between the day-to-day managing of a household and the care of God's church (1 Timothy 3:5). This implies much more than organizing a meeting. Paul goes on to speak of 'God's household, which is the church of the living God, the pillar and foundation of the truth' (1 Timothy 3:15). Like a human family, the church has a corporate identity and relationships stretching beyond those times when they are physically together. None of this means that the act of gathering is irrelevant. Regular meetings are important expressions of our identity and important occasions for building up the community. But too often church leaders focus on the meeting because this is what they do and what they know how to do.

Our view of church matters because what we understand by church is going to be hugely influential in our task of planting. If we think that church is primarily about the event of meeting, then the bulk of our effort will go into that event. We might be tempted to think that once that event is up and running, our job is more or less done. But church planting is about the long haul of seeing authentic, alternative communities created. George Hunsberger says,

> Churches are called to be bodies of people sent on a mission rather than the storefronts for vendors of religious services and goods . . . We must surrender the self-conception of the church as a voluntary association of individuals and live by the recognition that we are a communal body of Christ's followers, mutually committed and responsible to one another and to the mission Jesus set us upon at his resurrection.[10]

This is why we talk of church under the radar. People think they know what to expect when a new church opens. But when a group of people share their lives together as the people of God and get involved in blessing the city, then no-one is putting up defences. It's a 'stealth church'.

Mission by being good neighbours

Once upon a time a group of largely middle-class graduates in their mid-twenties moved into a deprived neighbourhood. Three made the move first and they were gradually joined by others. There are now ten in total, a combination of marrieds and singles, male and female. There is nothing remarkable about these people. None of them is hardcore or edgy. There is not even a tattoo among them as far as we are aware. Initially the plan was to plant a church. A lot of time was invested in recruiting leaders, but to no avail. For some time this failure to 'plant a church' was a cause of considerable frustration, animated conversation and earnest prayer.

But as this was going on, the Lord quietly got to work. How? Through these ordinary, unassuming individuals doing nothing more spectacular than being good neighbours. They were not a church – they attended a church elsewhere in the city. They did not hold meetings, did no formal evangelism, did not significantly change the way they spoke or dressed. They just lived there. All very ordinary and unspectacular. Nothing they did would have merited a mention in a missional church manual. But over a few years they have built credibility simply through being the neighbours everyone would want to have. They do have a corporate identity: they are known as 'the Christians'. That is because they share their lives, and are in and out of one another's homes. They sit out on the street in the summer and talk to people. They visit people in their homes, take dogs for walks, help with homework, assist with gardening. They bake, they mend and iron clothes. They go to the local pub and as regulars have started a weekly pub quiz. This has all led to helping a local couple get a café going, helping to organize a wedding for a local family and contributing to various birthday parties.

It has been interesting to watch how local people have responded. From the beginning the Christians were marked out as different. The way they spoke, the clothes they wore, their education and life choices all made them stand out. Single women in their late twenties and early thirties without children are unheard of in this area. At first there was misunderstanding. And indeed a degree of incomprehension remains, but they are trusted, respected and accepted. One day a block of houses opposite the home of some of these Christians was burnt down – a culmination of a long period of tension. And it was at the house of the Christians that people naturally congregated to discuss what to do as a street. People have become Christians through their witness and many others have heard the gospel.

The great thing about this story is that it enfranchises ordinary, run-of-the-mill, down-to-earth Christians like us. It opens up opportunities for gospel ministry to every church and every Christian. The group are now a church though the term is rarely used. This has turned out to be a case of church planting without even trying!

Mission by being good neighbours, good workers, good family members – that is what it's all about. In particular Peter calls us to a distinctive attitude toward others. We live in a culture where it is all about me: my rights, my pleasure, my fulfilment. God's people have an altogether different motto: 'It's not about me; it's about God and others.' That makes a profound difference when we enter the public square or the workplace or the home.

Peter's call to live good lives that commend the gospel is prefaced by a call to wage war against our sinful desires (2:11). And these are selfish desires. But Peter calls us away from self to serve others. This submission to others is not the end of self, but ironically its true fulfilment. Peter's teaching is subtly but powerfully subversive. He calls us to submit, literally, 'to every human creature' (2: 13–17). We submit to the king not because of his inherent authority but because he is an authority created by God. We honour the king but it is God we fear. Likewise Peter instructs slaves and wives when Greco-Roman ethical codes addressed only masters and husbands. Roman ethicists did not tell slaves to submit; they told masters to enforce submission. 'This direct instruction to slaves and wives implies that both have a measure of moral responsibility and choice unprecedented in Greek thought.'[11]

Yet from this radical position of freedom we offer submission: 'Live as free men, but do not use your freedom as a cover-up for evil; live as servants of God' (2:16). This beleaguered, ostracized, misunderstood Christian community is to respond by honouring everyone and treating everyone with respect. Our ethic is neither totalitarian nor individualistic, neither conformist nor fragmentary. Freedom is used to serve others in love (Galatians 5:13), or, as Paul puts it in 1 Corinthians 9:19, 'Though I am free and belong to no man, I make myself a slave to everyone, to win as many as possible.'

The film *Bobby* tells the story of Robert Kennedy's assassination in 1968. One scene involves a black chef named Edward Robinson (played by Laurence Fishburne). He is arguing with a Mexican waiter named Miguel as the staff eat a meal together in the kitchen. It is a time of racial tension and Miguel is angry at the injustice and prejudice he faces every day. He cannot understand why the chef is so laid-back and compliant. The chef responds, 'You know your problem, kid? You've got no poetry. You got no light. You got no one looking at you and saying, "Man! Look at Miguel. I want some of what he got."' Our life together as the people of God is a life of poetry and light created by the gospel. We are called to live a compelling shared life that makes others say, 'Man! Look at those Christians. I want what they got!'

In a society all too often characterized by demeaning insults or belittling humour or scathing comments, the Christian community is to treat everyone with dignity. Imagine the impact this might have in politics, schools and homes. Imagine the impact of honouring work colleagues, however unkind or incompetent or self-serving they may be. George Hunsberger says,

Because we live in a plural world that no longer gives us privileged place and power, we have the choice to confine our business to the private realm of self and its leisure choices or to find new patterns for faithful public deeds. The calling to seek first the reign of God and God's justice means orienting our public deeds away from imposing our moral will onto the social fabric, and toward giving tangible experience of the reign of God that intrudes as an alternative to the public principles and loyalties.[12]

'I wish there were more people like you.' That is what someone said recently to a member of my gospel community. We are called to be the people everyone would love to have as their neighbours. How do we thrive as God's people on the margins of society? How do we impact the people who despise and ridicule us? How do we answer the charges of our critics and accusers? How do we commend Jesus to our friends, family and neighbours? By living good and attractive lives.

We invest a lot in developing intellectual apologetic arguments and in training people who can deploy these arguments. We do not despise this at all. It has an important role to play. But 'it is God's will that by doing good you should silence the ignorant talk of foolish men' (2:15). It is easy to get intimidated by the likes of Richard Dawkins, Stephen Hawking, Christopher Hitchins or a colleague going on about the stupidity of Christians. But how do you silence them? By doing good.

> Faced by critics who want to carp and criticize? Don't answer back, just act: 'for it is God's will that by doing good you should silence the ignorant talk of foolish men' (1 Peter 2:15) . . . The truly Christian way of winning a good reputation for the gospel is for the local church to begin thinking seriously about what practical good can be done in its local community.[13]

I, Tim, am on the board of a local community forum. Some of the members can be quite vocal in their hostility to Christianity. They are among the cultural despisers of the faith. But when they learn that I am part of our church they have nothing but praise for what we are doing in the neighbourhood. The interesting thing is that our church is small and we do not run any big projects. At the last meeting the chair was commending the work done by different people in our church: clearing up rubbish, contributing to the residents' association, working with local shopkeepers, helping refugees. Emily and Wendy are two teenage girls who help with a local toddler group, making tea, bringing cakes, clearing up. You will not read about this sort of work in church planting manuals or mission textbooks. But people see it. Word gets back to me that unbelievers are impressed by what these girls are doing.

Gospel communities

1 Peter 3:15 is one of the more frustrating verses of the Bible: 'Always be prepared to give an answer to everyone who asks you to give the reason for the hope that you have.' It promises so much, especially to those of us in the silent majority of introverted non-evangelists. We want to share the gospel but many of us struggle to start gospel conversations. However, in this verse the focus is upon the other person to start the conversation as they ask us to explain our hope. Great!

The only problem is that this rarely happens. It is all too good to be true. What is at fault? Peter's expectations or our experience? A significant part of the problem is our failure to recognize the nature of pronouns. This is not a deficiency of grammar so much as a deficiency of culture. Those raised in a Western culture are almost bound to read the Bible individualistically because the culture is so aggressively individualistic. So every time we read 'you' we assume it means

'I'. But Peter means 'we', not simply because more than one person is being addressed, but because Peter is talking to his readers as a community. Verse 15 is the culmination of a line of thought that begins with Peter saying, 'Finally, all of you, live in harmony with one another; be sympathetic, love as brothers, be compassionate and humble' (3:8). In contrast to a self-serving society, we are to live in harmony. And it is this harmonious life together that will provoke the questions of verse 15. As we have already seen, the Old Testament descriptions of God's people that Peter alludes to in 2:9–10 evoke Israel's calling to witness to God through her corporate life. It is the good works of the church community and its life in the face of suffering that provoke questions about what we put our hope in and what we build identity around. Through exposure to the community of grace, people start to see that followers of Jesus are energized by something altogether different.

This means that, although we can do mission on our own, this should not be our primary strategy. We need to do it as part of missional community or, as we call them in our context, a gospel community, a group of people with a shared life and a shared mission. They have a common identity with a commitment to pastoring one another with the gospel and working together to witness to Christ in their context.

A gospel community can be a church in its own right or part of a larger congregation. So moving to gospel communities may not require a big change of structure. But it does requires a radical change of culture. A group of gospel communities that gathers together on Sunday mornings may look like a church with house groups, but the reality is very different. The gospel community is the core unit, the place where evangelism, pastoral care, discipleship and life take place.

Gospel communities are not like house groups, Bible study groups, pastoral groups or ministry teams. House groups obviously vary hugely and indeed yours may function very much like a gospel community. But let us paint the contrast in black and white to highlight the change in the culture that is required. House groups tend to be weekly. People talk about 'house group night' – the evening in which they 'do' house group by attending a meeting. A gospel community is a network of relationships, probably with a regular meeting, but also sharing life throughout the week. House groups are often centred upon a Bible study. In a gospel community the Bible is central but the Bible is read, discussed and lived throughout the week in the context of a shared life as well as through studies. House groups are often insular and focused on the mutual care of their members. Pastoral care is also a feature of gospel communities, but they are groups with a strong sense of mission too. They can articulate their vision for mission and identify the specific people they are trying to reach. House groups are normally managed centrally by the church leadership, and leaders can be fearful of house groups becoming independent. But gospel communities have a specific mandate to reproduce organically.

Missional focus
So one of the common characteristics of gospel communities is the missional focus or foci. They cannot reach everyone or contextualize to everyone, so they focus on reaching specific groups or communities. This helps the members to work together so that mission is a shared venture. Shared foci will usually emerge out of the passions of team members and the opportunities they encounter through the leading of the Holy Spirit, the great mission strategist.

We have found it helpful to make a distinction between

proactive and reactive intentionality. As a team we may have agreed a specific missional focus. But we still want to take in other gospel opportunities as they arise. Our lives will naturally bring us into contact with people who are not part of our focus. Indeed we may have opportunities while we are travelling with people with whom we cannot continue a relationship or connect with our gospel community. But we will still live our lives as witnesses of Jesus and still take opportunities to speak of him. This is reactive intentionality: we will be reactive to opportunities whenever and wherever they arise.

But where we can be proactive we will pursue our missional focus. Where we can make decisions about how we use our time, where we shop, with whom we eat and so on, we will do so in the light of our focus. This is proactive intentionality. Sometimes we can be proactive about the choice of our work. But other people will not be able to do this. They will spend their workdays being reactive to opportunities, but then make choices about what they do in the evenings and at weekends to pursue their missional focus.

One form that proactive intentionality can take is designating a time when the gospel community serves their neighbourhood together. One of our gospel communities sets aside one evening a week when everyone commits to doing mission together with the ethnic group they are trying to reach. They may invite people over for a film or visit people in local cafés. Another gospel community meets each Sunday morning for a short time of prayer. They then go out in groups to hang out with, or serve, unbelievers. Some go to the park to play football, while others host cookery sessions with young women. People are then invited back to a home for lunch together.

Our reactive intentionality means that new opportunities

for mission can open up in unexpected ways. So the missional focus may shift from time to time. Your missional focus is not always something you can lock down, and identifying your focus will often be an ongoing discussion. Alan Hirsch suggests the following questions to ask periodically to help evaluate your missional focus:[14]

1. Are we in close proximity with those we feel called to? Give example of proximity.
2. Are we spending regular time with these people? Give example of frequency.
3. Are we too busy to develop meaningful relationships? Give example of spontaneity.

The important thing is to set a culture in which people understand your values and vision so that they are free to respond to the leading of the Holy Spirit and do not need to refer to a plan or programme. Instead they are released to respond to opportunities as they emerge. The job of leaders is then to make sense of the chaos that results!

The following questionnaire is designed to give a snapshot of the health of a missional community using objective criteria. Do not use it as an occasion for discouragement or blame. Reflect on how together as a community you can take things forward rather than blaming other people ('them').

1. *How often do you have conversations with people in your missional community outside regular meetings?*
   once a month :: once a week :: twice a week :: more than twice a week
2. *How often are people from your missional community in your home or you in theirs?*

once a month :: once a week :: twice a week :: more than twice a week

3. *How often do people in your missional community talk about how the Holy Spirit has been speaking to them through God's Word?*
   once a month :: once a week :: twice a week :: more than twice a week

4. *How often do you talk with people in your missional community about your struggles to follow Jesus?*
   once a month :: once a week :: twice a week :: more than twice a week

5. *How often do unbelievers spend time with your missional community?*
   once a month :: once a week :: twice a week :: more than twice a week

6. *How often does your missional community spend time with unbelievers on their territory, in places where they feel comfortable?*
   hardly ever :: once a month :: once a week :: more than once a week

7. *Are the prayers of your missional community gospel-centred? Do you pray regularly for:*
   one another's godliness :: gospel opportunities :: boldness to speak of Christ :: the conversion of the lost :: the spread of the gospel around the world

8. *How many unbelievers are there with whom your missional community has regular conversations about Jesus or who are involved in Bible studies?*
   none :: one or two :: three or four :: many

9. *How many people in your missional community do your most significant unbelieving friends know by name?*
   none :: one or two :: about half of them :: most of them

10. *Would you bring your closest unbelieving friends to a typical get-together of your missional community?*

no :: in theory I would, but in reality I don't :: only if it's specifically designed around them :: yes

Turning the world upside down

When the apologists of the second and third centuries were defending Christianity they pointed to the lives of the Christians as their strongest argument for giving it freedom. These men and women saw themselves as a third race, neither Jew nor Gentile. They lived as free men and women and used their freedom to do good. This is how the early church 'turned the world upside down' (Acts 17:6 ESV).

Commenting on the dramatic growth of the church during the first centuries after Christ, Rodney Stark, the American social scientist, points out that there was no great strategy, no mass communication and there were no leading personalities.[15] Yet the gospel spread and churches sprang up all across the empire. By the middle of the second century Justinus said, 'There is not a race of men on the earth among whom converts to the Christian faith cannot be found.'[16] By the end of that century Tertullian could say, 'We came on the scene only yesterday and already we fill all your institutions, your towns, walled cities, your fortresses . . . your senate and your forum.'[17]

Alan Hirsch asks how the early Christians managed this rate of expansion when they were an illegal religion with no church buildings, no Bibles in the hands of ordinary believers, no professional leadership, no youth groups, no worship bands, no seminaries and no commentaries. And they even made it hard to join the church.

Perhaps some of these factors were not impediments to growth, but assisted the spread of the gospel. Growth was not restricted by buildings or clergy. This was a grassroots movement of ordinary men and women doing everyday church and everyday mission. The constant threat of persecution, suggests Hirsch, drove 'the persecuted to live very close to their message – they simply cling to the gospel of Jesus and thus unlock its liberating power'.[18]

Stark argues that Christianity grew because of the way it cared for people, both within and outside the church. He claims that two widespread epidemics during this period played a particularly significant role. The church could not do major social projects such as cleaning up the streets so you might still have a dead body rotting in the sewer that ran down the middle of the road. But Christians cared for one another, leading to greater survival rates. This in turn led to an increased proportion of Christians in urban centres, which meant that more people's lives intersected with networks of Christians at a time when traditional social bonds were being disrupted by the epidemics. Christians also cared for non-Christians, bringing the latter into the sphere of Christian influence and commending the faith to pagans. Stark cites a number of pagan sources complaining about the good reputation Christians were gaining. Pagan priests fled for their lives while Christians were sustained by a more enduring hope. The church historian Henry Chadwick says,

> The practical application of charity was probably the most potent single cause of Christian success. The pagan comment: 'See how these Christians love each other' (reported by Tertullian) was not irony. Christian charity expressed itself in care for the poor, for widows and orphans, in visits to brethren in prison or condemned to death in labour mines, and social action in time of calamity like famine, earthquake, pestilence, or war.[19]

Stark also draws attention to the distinctive way in which the church treated women. Most pagan girls were married off before puberty with little say in the matter. Christian women had plenty of say and tended to marry around the age of eighteen. Abortion was also a huge killer of women in this period but Christian women were spared this. Pagans routinely practised infanticide. Indeed archaeologists have discovered sewers clogged with the bones of newborn girls. Not only did Christians prohibit this, but they would also rescue abandoned infants and bring them into their own families. Female infanticide and mortality during abortions meant that men outnumbered women in the Roman Empire. Not so in the church. As a result, fertility rates among Christians were higher, which itself contributed to an increase in the proportion of Christians in the Empire.

Christianity prospered in a culture in which you cared only for your tribe. Popular entertainment involved watching people being tortured and killed in the arena while you shouted, 'Shake him! Jump up and down on him.' In contrast, claims Stark, what Christianity gave to its converts was nothing less than their humanity.[20]

This is what Peter is talking about. In the face of persecution or the threat of persecution, ordinary Christians took the gospel the length and breadth of the Roman Empire.

It's not complicated, though, of course, living differently by grace is never easy. God has not equipped us all to be big personalities with multiple gifts or oratory that draws the crowds. But through the death of Christ and the faithful work of the Spirit he has empowered us all to live such good lives that others are drawn to Christ. However you 'do' church, let it be nothing less than the people of God on mission together. We are a city on a hill and a light to the world.

5. EVERYDAY EVANGELISM

1 Peter 3:15–16

But in your hearts set apart Christ as Lord. Always be prepared to
give an answer to everyone who asks you to give the reason for the
hope that you have. But do this with gentleness and respect, keeping
a clear conscience, so that those who speak maliciously against your
good behaviour in Christ may be ashamed of their slander.
(3:15–16)

Some people are natural evangelists. They somehow always
seem to get into gospel conversations. They go into a shop,
sit on the bus, stand in a queue and end up talking about
Jesus. We do not know how they do it. Indeed most of the
time they themselves do not really know how they do it. It
just seems to happen.

Neither of us is like that. We wish we were. We have to

work out how to evangelize. So our best course is to make merit of our deficiency and work out some ideas for sharing the gospel that others who are not natural evangelists can use.

So how can we talk about Jesus in the context of everyday life?

The first way is to do everyday pastoral care. Think of your Christian friends as guinea pigs – an opportunity to practise! If you find it hard to talk about Jesus with Christians then how do you expect to talk about him with unbelievers? As you get more into the habit of talking about Jesus with Christians you may well find it easier to talk about him with unbelievers. The links between everyday life and Jesus will become easier to spot. Let your unbelieving friends overhear you 'gospelling' one another. We're not talking about stage-managed conversations – people will see through that straightaway. We mean exposing people to a community that is genuinely centred on Jesus. As people come into this community they will hear the gospel being spoken around them.

We want to suggest some tools, some approaches for talking about the gospel with your unbelieving friends. In many ways, these are the same as those used for everyday pastoral care, but this time with unbelievers in view. That is because in both pastoral care and evangelism we have both the same content and the same context: the content is the gospel and the context is everyday life.

Evangelism in a post-Christian culture
Many current evangelistic approaches assume a Christian culture, but, as we have seen, we live in an increasingly post-Christian culture. People are biblically illiterate and do not start with the basics of a Christian worldview. Guilt, faith, sin, God are all empty or confused concepts. Unbelievers will not be converted through a ten-minute gospel presentation

on the back of a serviette. They need a lot of nudging, a lot of gaps filling in. Or they start with a deep-seated antipathy towards Christianity. They are not going to welcome a four-point gospel presentation, however well practised it may be.

If we could place people on a range of one to ten depending on their interest in the gospel (with one being no interest and ten being a decision to follow Christ) we would find that lots of evangelism assumes that people are at around eight. We teach our gospel outlines, our answers to apologetic questions. We hold guest services. We put on evangelistic courses. We preach in the open air or knock on doors. All great things to do, but 70% of the population are at one or two.

Many of us know how to answer the question: 'What must I do to be saved?' But we do not know how to *begin* a conversation about Jesus. Our only hope is a crass, awkward change of direction like crunching the gears in your car. So you are watching football and you resort to saying things like: 'At last a substitution. Did you know that Jesus could be your substitute?' 'Great goal. What about you? What's the goal of your life?' 'Come on referee – that was never a penalty! Did you know Jesus paid the penalty of our sin?'

Here are a couple of implications.

First, we need to be patient and trust God's sovereignty. As often as not, our role is to move someone one or two steps along the way rather than get them all the way to number ten in one go. God is in control of mission, sovereign in salvation. Trust him to take the little morsel of the gospel message you give someone and use it as part of his purposes in their life. 'Make the most of every opportunity,' says Paul in Colossians 4:5, not 'make opportunities'. Our role is to live good and attractive lives under the lordship of Christ, lives that provoke questions (1 Peter 3:15–16).

And sometimes less is more. We often find that when we

are sharing the gospel along with another Christian we wish they would shut up more. They seem desperate to fill the silence. We need to give people time to think. We are asking them to believe a totally different worldview full of weird and miraculous concepts. We are asking them to make a life-changing decision. At least give them a chance to think before you unload another heap of strange ideas on them. Trust the Holy Spirit, the ultimate Evangelist, to work on their hearts. He and he alone persuades people of the truth, convicting of sin, righteousness and judgment. He opens blind eyes, melts hard hearts. And the wonderful thing about the Holy Spirit is that his pace is always right. While you are silent the Holy Spirit is at work and he will gently but surely accomplish what God purposes in a person's life.

So when we get a gospel opportunity we do not have to run through the full presentation. At best that will be too much information. At worst you may ensure unbelievers never ask you about anything 'religious' for fear they get the twenty-minute version again.

Secondly, we need to find ways of presenting the gospel at points one and two on our scale of interest in Christ and not just at points eight and nine.

We typically train people to answer the most frequently asked apologetic questions, such as: 'Why does God allow suffering?' and 'What about other religions?' The problem is that these lists of 'top' questions are self-selecting. They are not actually the most commonly asked questions. They exclude the real questions people ask, such as: 'Where are my car keys?' and 'What do you think about this dress?' We cannot wait for people to ask the metaphysical questions. We need to identify gospel responses to the 'mundane'.

But how can we do this? We want to suggest four points of intersection and four liberating truths that might help us to use presenting issues as windows to the heart. This approach affirms much that people are already doing as well as bringing some focus and edge to evangelism.

1. Four points of intersection

We are all interpreters. God made us to make sense of life. So human beings are always looking to interpret it. We were made to live trusting in God's Word, for God's Word is the interpretation that brings wholeness and sanity to our lives. But of course there are other interpreters and other interpretations too. Human rebellion began when Eve listened to another interpreter (Satan) and another interpretation (that God is a tyrant whose rule should be rejected).

Take a five-minute snapshot of an office or someone's living room and you will hear people trying to make sense of their own experiences. And we look to one another for interpretation or for our own interpretations to be confirmed. This is what the Bible calls 'the world' – collective reinterpretations of life that shape us and to which we contribute.

Opportunities often arise when a person's interpretation of life begins to break down. And any view of life not governed by God's Word is going to fail at some point. A problem or crisis in a friend's life is a moment of exposure.

For example, if our interpretation of life is one of self-reliance then cracks will appear when life becomes difficult or events overtake us. We begin to realize that we do not control our circumstances. Sickness, death, disaster become a glaring reminder to us that relying on ourselves does not work.

Or if our interpretation of life is to look to others to satisfy us then cracks will appear when people let us down. Loneliness, disappointment and resentment will become a glaring reminder that relying on others does not work.

Or if we have interpreted life as a series of events in which we are to be satisfied then the cracks will appear when each fix begins to fail us. We become desperate for another drink, another relationship, another plate of food, another holiday. Our desires become more focused or our efforts more obsessive, and eventually the reality of our enslavement becomes public.

Or if we have interpreted life as striving to be perfect then cracks will appear in those moments when we cannot sustain perfection. We will start to cover up our faults, lies will creep in or we will hide from people whose opinions we value. We will develop strategies to make us look more beautiful or clever or kind. We are trying to justify ourselves but we cannot be justified by our works.

Sometimes a person's interpretation of life breaks down when they are successful. They achieve all that they had ever hoped to achieve, but then find that it is not enough. They still feel empty, longing for more. Of course, we are made to know God so a new spouse, a successful career, a beautiful home, material prosperity will all end up being poor substitutes.

Everyone has a gospel story

The primary way in which we interpret life is through stories and *everyone has a gospel story*. Everyone. Everyone has their version of salvation which is a 'gospel' story in that it purports to offer good news. In other words, there are secular gospels as well as religious gospels.

We can use the framework of creation, fall, redemption and consummation or new creation as four points of intersection: four points at which people's stories intersect with the true gospel story. Obviously people do not use the categories above. But they will talk about who they are and what they are meant to be (creation). They will talk about what is wrong with them or what is wrong with the world: somebody or something will be blamed (fall). They will also have a sense of what needs to happen for things to be put right (redemption) and some sense of the state of affairs that they are hoping will give them meaning or satisfaction (consummation).

Creation	My identity
Fall	My problem
Redemption	My solution
Consummation	My hope

In Genesis 3 God's word is reinterpreted by the serpent as follows:

Creation	You are meant to be gods.
Fall	You are held back by God and his insecurities.
Redemption	You can be set free by disobeying God.
Consummation	You will be gods.

Despite this rejection of God's word and God's rule, in God's grace the Bible story becomes:

Creation	We are made in God's image to reflect his glory, to love God and love others.
Fall	We have rebelled against God's rule, but our self-rule leads to conflict, slavery and judgment.
Redemption	God restores his rule by sending his Son and graciously enables us to live under his rule by paying the price of our judgment on the cross.

Consummation   God will recreate this broken world when
                 Jesus returns.

There are actually lots of ways you could tell this story.
While there are clearly some wrong ways of telling the gospel
story, you can define creation, fall, redemption and consummation in a variety of biblical ways which will connect
more or less directly to the people with whom you are
talking.

Consider this snippet of conversation: 'I'm leaving Jane
because she's not prepared to see my point of view.' It suggests the following 'gospel story':

Creation   I should be in control or sovereign.
Fall   Other people prevent me from being
                  sovereign.
Redemption   I will avoid people who challenge my
                  sovereignty.
Consummation   My sovereignty is unchallenged.

But this story is never going to offer good news because
it leads to broken relationships. The Bible's gospel story
is:

Creation   We are made to find freedom under
                  God's sovereignty.
Fall   We rejected God's sovereignty in favour
                  of self-sovereignty (so this person's
                  solution is actually the problem).
Redemption   God welcomes rebels back under his
                  sovereignty through the cross.
Consummation   God will restore his liberating rule over
                  the world.

Everyone is trying to find salvation. They might not ask, 'What must I do to be saved?' But everyone has some sense of what it is that would make them fulfilled, satisfied, accepted. Think about the people you know. Think about yourself.

   1. How do they define salvation? How will they know they've arrived? *'I'll be happy, fulfilled, accepted if . . .'*

   2. What must they do to be saved? What law or rules must they follow? *'To achieve this I've got to . . .'*

What these questions highlight is that some (religious) people are pursuing a right understanding of salvation by the wrong means, trying to be reconciled with God through their own good works. Others are pursuing a wrong understanding of salvation. It might be marriage, a liberated homeland, success in business, the acceptance of friends, a happy family, a beautiful home, the admiration of men, the worship of women, a wonderful holiday, prosperity or security. Or they may be pursuing their secular version of salvation through their own form of legalism. They too have a law to which they must conform to be successful or to find meaning. And their justification by works is no more successful than that of the religious legalist. On a good day they will feel proud of their achievements and look down on others. But on a bad day they will be crushed. And because they are pursuing a wrong vision of redemption, even when they are successful they are left feeling empty and unfulfilled. As Tim Keller says, 'Jesus is the only Lord who, if you receive him, will fulfil you completely, and, if you fail him, will forgive you eternally.'[1]

Another window on to a person's 'gospel story' is their view of other people. Legalists routinely 'rank' people because life is a ladder on which they climb towards redemption and by which they assess how well they are doing in relation to those above and below them. So the person someone looks up to will epitomize their view of salvation and consummation. If they idolize wealthy people then they may well see salvation as prosperity. If they idolize cool people then they may see salvation as acceptance. And the behaviour they condemn will be the reverse of what they consider to be the means of redemption. So if they condemn idleness then they may well see hard work as the means to salvation. If they condemn people who look uncool then they may see the latest fashions as the means of salvation.

Here are questions that help to reveal a person's gospel story:

Creation:	What do they assume the world should be like? What kind of a person would they like to be? Who are their heroes? What would have to be in place for them to feel happy?
Fall:	How do they describe their struggles and battles? What do they feel is their most pressing problem? What do they feel they lack? Who or what do they think is responsible?
Redemption:	What do they think will make life better? What provides a sense of escape or release? Who or what will deliver their hopes? What are their functional saviours?
Consummation:	What are their hopes? What is the long-term project to which they are working? What are the dreams for which they make sacrifices? Have they given up so that their hope has now shrunk simply to getting through the day?

People are expressing their versions of the creation story or the fall or redemption or consummation *all the time*. Reflect on a recent conversation you have had with an unbeliever. Can you identify any comments expressing alternative creation, fall, redemption and consummation stories? How might you have used these moments to speak about the gospel story?

What we are looking for are points of intersection. As we begin to identity the creation, fall, redemption, consummation narrative of a person's life, so we can begin to relate these to the Bible's gospel story. Sometimes you may challenge a person's worldview, but look out too for opportunities to affirm links between what a person is saying and the Bible story. Most of the time we will not get the opportunity to do the full four episodes. On one occasion we might get people thinking about the true problem they face in life while on another we may get the chance to highlight the way self-justification does not work.[2]

Case study: the slimmer's gospel

Jonny Woodrow, one of our leaders in The Crowded House, has been attending a slimming programme for a couple of years. He identifies 'the slimmer's gospel' as follows:

Creation	I'm meant to be happy and valued.
Fall	I'm not physically attractive enough because I'm overweight.
Redemption	I can change through will-power, weight loss and exercise.
Consummation	I hope that my body will be transformed because then I'll be appreciated.

Along the way there are lots of signs of sanctification: dress sizes and weekly weigh-ins for example. At meetings there are testimonies – the organizers want you to bring in your now over-sized clothes. You even sit around 'the book' identifying right(eous) and unrighteous foods. At its simplest, the slimmer's gospel is: 'I want to be accepted and I can be accepted if I follow the rules.' It is justification by works. It gives us an opportunity to speak of justification by grace.

Jonny articulates the *gospel* slimmer's gospel as follows:

Creation	I'm meant to enjoy God and enjoy his good gifts.
Fall	I use God's gift of food to replace God and find myself enslaved by food and filled with shame.
Redemption	Jesus restores me by offering his body in my place and he invites me to a meal with him.
Consummation	I can find lasting satisfaction in Jesus, the bread of life, so that I'm liberated from my need for refuge in food.

The following is a real conversation about food with labels added, identifying how different statements reflect the four intersecting moments.

'Wouldn't it be easier if we didn't have food?' (*Creation*)

'Why do you say that?'

'Well, it just causes health problems and weight gain. I've never got on with it!' (*Fall*)

'What's your struggle with it?' (*Fall*)

'I like it too much! I've dieted on and off but at my age it gets harder to lose weight.' (*Failed redemption*)

'Have you always struggled with food?' (*Fall*)

'I guess I'm a comfort eater really.' (*Redemption*)

'It's a bit of a refuge for you?' (*Redemption*)

'I get in from work and hit the chocolate.' (*Redemption*)

'So you have a love-hate relationship with it. I don't think anyone has a real handle on how to relate to food. We're all mixed up about it.' (*Fall*)

'Yeah, just look at celebrities. Always yoyo dieting! All that money and they still can't be satisfied.' (*Failed redemption*)

'Would you feel better about food if you could just get on top of your diet?' (*Redemption*)

'Yeah, but no-one's on top of their diet.' (*Fall*)

'No, I guess that's why there are so many makeover shows on TV. I think it's because we're not supposed to use food to feel better about life. It just doesn't work, does it?' (*Failed redemption*)

'No, I guess it's not worked for me at least.' (*Failed redemption*)

'Food is a good thing, but we use it to hide. So it messes us up. (*Creation and fall*) We get addicted to it and use it to control our lives. (*Redemption*) The Bible says that God made food as a good gift to be enjoyed. But the first woman turned to food to make herself feel like she was someone. Ever since, we've turned to food instead of God to get satisfied and make ourselves feel better about ourselves ... But Jesus said he was bread from heaven! He's the only one who truly satisfies.' (*Gospel*)

2. Four liberating truths

Many people today do not feel a big sense of guilt. And the guilt of falling short of God's law is not a feature of their thinking. There may be moments when they feel the need of forgiveness but generally they do not have a strong sense of being sinners. But they do feel trapped, unable to be the people they want to be. And the Bible has a compelling and persuasive explanation for this – and good news of a way out.

We know that the source of all human behaviour and emotions is the heart. In the Western world we think with our heads and feel with our hearts. But in the Bible the heart represents the totality of our inner selves. We think, feel, hope, desire, love, fear with our hearts. Proverbs 4:23 says:

> Above all else, guard your heart,
>   for it is the wellspring of life.

The heart signifies our motivational core: our lives, our words, our actions, our emotions are the outflow (Mark 7:20–23; Luke 6:43–45; Romans 1:21–25; Ephesians 4:17–24; James 4:1–10). Circumstances, upbringing, hormones and our personal history all play a part in shaping our behaviour, but the root problem is the sinful desires of the heart (James 1:13–15). Destructive behaviour and negative emotions arise when we do not see God as the source of all that is good and so desire or worship other things in his place. And a sinful desire is not just a desire for a bad thing. It can also be a desire for a good thing which has become bigger than God.

This unbelief and idolatry leads to slavery (John 8:34–36). The thing that our hearts treasure or worship will be the thing that controls our lives (Matthew 6:21, 24). 'A man is a slave to whatever has mastered him' (2 Peter 2:19). We feel trapped, as if we cannot change. And in one sense we cannot. Trying to change behaviour alone does not work because we are not free to change. We need God to set us free through the truth.

This offers a point of connection with people, a hook, an opportunity to engage. The gospel is good news of freedom from the enslavement to the addictive behaviour and negative emotions created by sinful desires. Jesus says, 'The truth will set you free' (John 8:31–34). Just as lies about God lead to the slavery of sin, so the truth about God leads to the freedom of service (Galatians 5:1, 13). If I am enslaved by my worries then freedom is found in trusting the sovereign care of my heavenly Father. If I am enslaved by the need to prove myself then freedom is found in trusting that I am fully justified in God's sight through the atoning work of Christ.

Because these lies and idolatrous desires create slavery, when we proclaim the truth or call them to worship the living God, we are offering *good news.*

This approach engages with the specifics of people's lives. And people are more likely to engage with the particular issues that affect their lives: anger, bitterness, parenting, shopping, addiction, economic need, depression, violence and so on. We can do more than deal with these issues *as a context* for speaking the gospel. Instead we can treat these presenting issues as windows on to heart issues. We need to connect the gospel with specifics rather than, or as well as, starting with big metaphysical questions.

This is not just addressing felt needs. It takes you right where you want to go. Indeed a weakness of some approaches to evangelism is that they present ideas for intellectual assent. And people can sign up to a set of ideas (believing Jesus died for their sins and rose again), but the idolatrous desires of their heart remain untouched. Their motivational framework is unchanged and true repentance has not taken place.

When we use presenting issues as a window to the heart, we are in effect contextualizing the gospel on a person-by-person basis, identifying the particular sinful desires that control a person's life and the particular truths that will set them free.

Case study: the rich young ruler in Luke 18
Imagine you are asked: 'What must I do to have eternal life?' Would you ever dream of saying, 'Spend your life serving the

poor'? Most of us would regard such a response as suspect, heretical even. It smacks of salvation by works. Yet this is what Jesus says to a rich young man in Luke 18:18–25.

'What must I do to have eternal life?' is a gift of a question. Surely the answer would be a model gospel outline. But the response of Jesus does not look anything like 'Two Ways To Live'. Jesus does not draw a diagram with the cross bridging the chasm between us and God. Instead Jesus commands this young man to give his money to the poor.

The reason is that this command goes right to the heart of this man's problem: his idolatrous desires. His desire for wealth and security controls him. A man who worships money is called to repent of his idolatry and express that repentance in concrete ways. This is just what happens a short time later. When Zacchaeus declares, 'Look, Lord! Here and now I give half of my possessions to the poor, and if I have cheated anybody out of anything, I will pay back four times the amount', Jesus responds, 'Today salvation has come to this house' (Luke 19:8–9).

Case study: the woman at the well in John 4
Jesus promises the Samaritan woman at the well (John 4) living water that will truly satisfy. Then he asks her to fetch her husband. It looks like a tangent. But it leads straight to her heart. She says she has no husband to fetch. Jesus knows she has had five husbands and the man with whom she is now is not her husband. This woman has been looking for meaning, satisfaction and fulfilment in marriage, sex and intimacy. But they are like water that leaves her thirsty again. No doubt there was real pleasure. But it did not last.

She tries to change the subject with her question about worship, but again Jesus uses this to go to the heart of the issue. The question is not *where* you worship, but *what* you worship. She was trying to find satisfaction from a man instead of from God and in the process made an idol of sexual intimacy. The maths tell the story: five husbands plus another man. What are the patterns in people's lives? Are the words 'If only . . .' a refrain ?

Jesus, of course, has supernatural knowledge of her heart and her history. But we need not despair. We can get to know people as we share our lives with them. We can ask questions. We can ask for insight from the Holy Spirit. Plus, as with pastoral care, we do not have to get our analysis spot on before we speak the gospel.

The fact that this woman comes to the well at noon gives her away. You do not do the hard work of drawing water at the hottest time of day! But she does not want to draw water in the morning when the other women are around. She lives a life of shame. But her encounter with Jesus transforms that. After meeting Jesus we are told: 'The woman went back to the town and said to the people, "Come, see a man who told me everything I ever did. Could this be the Christ?"' (John 4:28–29). The shame and hiding are over. Jesus knew all that she had done and still he offered her living water. That is freedom indeed.

Proclaiming liberating truth
The four liberating truths that provided a framework for everyday pastoral care also provide a framework for everyday evangelism. They help to identify the underlying unbelief and idolatry behind people's behaviour as well as pointing to the truth that will set them free.

1. God is great – so we don't have to be in control
2. God is glorious – so we don't have to fear others
3. God is good – so we don't have to look elsewhere
4. God is gracious – so we don't have to prove ourselves

All of these truths are good news. As you talk with someone you can ask yourself which of these four truths they are failing to believe. Then you can begin to think about how you can speak that truth into their situation.

Consider, for example, someone who is over-busy, stressed and worn out. How might a failure to believe one or more of these four truths be the root cause?

- They might be too busy because they are insecure and need to control life, but God is great and cares for us as a sovereign heavenly Father.
- They might be too busy because they fear other people and so they cannot say no, but God is glorious and his opinion is the one that really matters.
- They might be too busy because they are filling their lives with activity in a desperate attempt to find satisfaction, but God is good and he's the true source of joy.
- They might be too busy because they are trying to prove themselves through their work, but God is gracious and justifies us freely through faith in the finished work of Christ.

Putting it into practice

Identify generative themes. 'Generative themes' is a term borrowed from the Brazilian educationalist Paulo Freire who developed an approach to teaching literacy built around the issues that generated energy in a community. These issues mattered to people and so motivated their learning. Look for topics that generate energy, that make people excited, angry, agitated or enthusiastic. These are often windows on to the things about which they care deeply.

Reinsert God into the picture. Typically people leave God

out of the picture when they talk about their lives. So deliberately reinsert him into what you are saying. Take the sentence: 'I just can't say "no" to John.' What does the interpretation reveal? 'My life has meaning and joy only when I have John's approval. John is the one who lights up my life; he's my light and my salvation. John has become an idol: a god-like figure who makes life full and complete.' Now what belief about God does that reveal? Insert God into the picture. 'John matters more than God, or John gives more joy than God can give. I desire or worship or treasure John more than God.'

Powerful questions. As we have noted already, Jesus had supernatural knowledge which enabled him to see the idolatrous desires and enslaving beliefs of people's hearts. Most of the time we cannot do this (although sometimes the Holy Spirit gives us special discernment). Instead we can ask questions.[3]

At a conversational level, a good question to ask is, **'What do you want?'** As someone explains a situation and perhaps seeks your advice, ask what it is they want, their ideal outcome?

You can then ask, **'Why?'** 'Why does it matter so much to you?' begins to push beyond the outcomes they want to the underlying idolatrous desires of their heart. The 'Why?' question also helps you to move beyond 'surface idols' (like a new car) to identify 'deep idols' (like respect) so it becomes clear which of the four liberating truths comes into play.[4]

Asking 'What do you want?' and 'Why?' is a simple approach that can create a platform to share the four liberating truths as good news. 'I just want the children to pick up their laundry,' someone might say. Nothing wrong with that. But if this is generating energy and conflict then maybe there is more to it. Push a bit further and it might become clear that they want a part of their life that is under their control; they want to be god in their home. The good news is that God is great, he is in control and his control can be trusted.

Of course repeatedly asking 'Why? Why? Why?' might make you sound like an annoying four-year-old. But you do not have to do it all in one go. You can explore issues over successive conversations as opportunities arise. Remember that God is the great orchestrator of mission. We need not 'close the deal' every time. When that appropriate point comes, we may or may not be involved. But we can trust God to organize the route.

Mission involves a multiplicity of activities, such as sharing meals, helping with chores, hanging out, doing recreational activities, answering questions, sharing snippets of gospel truth, engaging in conversations that appear to go nowhere. On their own most of these may not look like mission. But if you persevere with prayer and gospel intentionality then God will use them in his purposes.

Another helpful question is, **'How's that working for you?'** In other words, what are the results in your life of living for this (your functional god)? In times of crisis it will become clear that people's functional gods do not deliver.

In conversation with people bear in the mind the following questions. You may not ask them straight out but they may influence the direction of your conversation.

- What do they believe (or not believe) about God?
- What do they want? What are their idolatrous desires?
- How do these idolatrous desires control their lives?
- Which of the four liberating truths is most relevant to their situation (the greatness, glory, grace or goodness of God)?

Adapting typical modes of conversation

We can also adapt common modes of discourse. Here we highlight four that cry out for gospel responses.

Turning confirmation into reinterpretation. People are often looking for their interpretations to be confirmed. They may make a statement in a manner that invites a response. Or they may pose it as a question. Little questions that pepper people's discourses are invitations to reinterpret what they are saying according to the gospel story. Isn't that right? (The phrase 'Isn't that right' being a common example of what we are talking about.) The slang term 'innit' is a gospel opportunity for it represents a request to have an interpretation of the world confirmed.

Turning advice into proclamation. People are often looking for advice: 'What would you do?', 'Which of these do I look best in?' This advice-seeking is an opportunity. If someone is asking you what shirt to wear, tell them to wear the blue one. We are not suggesting some weird twisting of the conversation (e.g. 'You should clothe yourself with Jesus'). But the advice of others is most people's primary source of ideas and influence. When they face tough choices they ask their friends. It is very easy to get drawn into giving advice. But this is often also an opportunity to proclaim Christ.

'Should I go out with him?' a woman might say. 'Why would you ask that question if you are not sure you love him? Is it because you need a boyfriend in order to feel complete? If you expect some bloke to make you feel that way then you're going to be disappointed, for you were made to know God.'

Turning complaint into lament. One common form of discourse is moaning. 'Whenever my friends get together we start by moaning to one another,' someone told me recently. Christians can interpret this as ungodliness. And maybe it is. But maybe we can also associate it with the biblical category of lament. We declare what is wrong with the world. In terms of our four intersecting moments these are 'fall' statements. We can perhaps also begin to declare gospel hope for that sinful world.

Turning anecdote into testimony. When most people get together they tell stories, not big narratives or well-constructed tales, but anecdotes: 'Do you know what my boss said to me today?' 'I was down town this morning.' 'You'll never guess who I met on the way here.' 'The weirdest thing happened to me on holiday last year.'

This basic mode of conversation is a great opportunity to testify to God's work in our lives. We need to rediscover the power of testimony. By this we do not necessarily mean telling the story of how you became a Christian; it is a great thing to do, but the opportunity for it will be rare. What we mean is testifying to the power of the four liberating truths by relating how one of these has helped you in your life. This allows you to proclaim the truth in a non-confrontational manner – indeed people find it hard to refute another person's story. It also allows you to speak of your own brokenness, together with God's redeeming grace, in a way that disarms people's assumption that Christianity is legalism or that Christians think themselves morally superior. So people might not often ask, 'Tell me how you became a Christian.' But you will get opportunities to say, 'I once faced a similar problem and the thing that kept me going was knowing that my Father in heaven was looking after me.' 'Do you know what my boss said to me today? . . . I had to tell myself that God's opinion was what mattered, not Mr Smith's!'

Let us go back to the questions we highlighted as examples of real frequently asked questions: 'Where are my car keys?' 'What do you think about this dress?' Most of the time the appropriate answers will be: 'On the kitchen counter' and

'You look great in it.' But there may also be moments when you can go further: 'Why do you always get so agitated when you lose your keys?' It could be because this person wants life to be under their control. The good news is that God is great. Or it could be that they are afraid of being late because they fear other people's opinion. The good news is that God is glorious and that his is the opinion that really matters. Or you might ask, 'Why does looking good matter so much to you?' 'How's that working for you with all your credit card debts?' It could be that this person sees salvation in terms of acceptance, and the 'law' by which they are trying to justify themselves is looking cool. The good news is that God is gracious, so we are accepted by grace through the finished work of Christ.

The next step

And what is the next step? Exposure to the Christian community. Here people will not only hear the gospel word, but see it being loved and lived out. They will see the power of the gospel to unite disparate people and make them family. And they will also see us failing and falling out, but then see grace in action. They will hear our message with a variety of voices and from a variety of experiences. The different gifts God has given us will work together to create a compelling testimony to gospel.

By exposure to the Christian community we mean being introduced to the network of relationships that make up the church, sharing in the life of the community in the context of everyday life. Often people will dismiss our intellectual arguments but they will find it much harder to dismiss the compelling witness of the Christian community: 'Live such good lives among the pagans that, though they accuse you of doing wrong, they may see your good deeds and glorify God on the day he visits us' (2:12).

6. HOPE AT THE MARGINS

1 Peter 3:8 – 5:14

'Dear friends, do not be surprised at the painful trial you are suffering, as though something strange were happening to you. But rejoice that you participate in the sufferings of Christ, so that you may be overjoyed when his glory is revealed' (1 Peter 4:12–13). Peter's readers certainly knew what it meant to live at the margins of society. His letter is full of references to suffering, rejection and persecution. But it is also full of references to hope. The perspective of Christian hope changes everything. It changes our attitudes to living on the margins. It changes our attitudes to our time, money and careers, freeing up resources for mission.

In all the contemporary talk of missional church and the plethora of cutting-edge strategies for reaching people with the gospel, little attention has been given to the issue of persecution. It is easy to understand why. Many people are familiar with Tertullian's (c. 160–220 AD) famous aphorism that 'the blood of the martyrs is the seed of the church'. But we are reluctant to take it too seriously. It is one of those soundbites that we are happy to recite, but only because we are not in northern Africa in the second century facing another onslaught from the Roman Empire.

Yet even a cursory look at church history should give us cause to take note. Consider two relatively recent examples. In China the Cultural Revolution (1966–1976) banned any expression of religious life. Believers were imprisoned and sometimes tortured. Bibles were destroyed, churches looted and Christians subjected to humiliation. In the 1980s thousands were again imprisoned. Yet now there are an estimated 40 million Protestant Christians in China, perhaps many more. In Cambodia there were around 10,000 church members when the Khmer Rouge assumed control in 1975. Missionaries were forced to leave and the persecution of the church was savage. Ninety per cent of Christians and all Christian leaders were martyred or exiled. Hundreds of thousands of Cambodians fled to refugee camps in Thailand. Yet despite the Khmer Rouge's attempt to crush it, the Cambodian church survived and grew. Today it is growing with around 40,000 believers and 750 churches. Peter Wagner once claimed that church planting is the most effective evangelistic strategy. But the evidence suggests that we should perhaps modify this claim: it's persecution which is the most effective evangelistic strategy.

So we end where we began: at the margins. Painful trials are normal. We should expect suffering.

Peter says: 'In this you greatly rejoice, though now for a little while you may have had to suffer grief in all kinds of trials' (1:6). We rejoice greatly, not only in the face of trials but also in the midst of grief. What a strange and disconcerting paradox! In our culture grief and joy are incompatible. But biblically they can co-exist. Grief in response to our circumstances does not overcome joy because circumstances do not threaten our inheritance. Tears cannot extinguish joy.

So what is the source of this joy? Peter highlights a number of interconnected truths that feed this unusual response: the association with our Saviour, the care of our Father, the support of our church family and, most prominent of all, the hope of glory.

The association with the Saviour

Peter stresses that the suffering he is talking about arises from our connection to Christ and from doing good in his name (2:18–21; 3:13–17; 4:14–16). 'If you suffer as a Christian, do not be ashamed, but praise God that you bear that name' (4:16). But he is also doing something more. Peter repeatedly refers in his letter to the sufferings of Christ (1:11; 2:21; 2:23; 2:24; 3:18; 4:1; 4:13; 5:1). As Christians we follow a Saviour who suffered so we too must expect to suffer, and indeed our sufferings are a participation in the sufferings of Christ. Our ability to rejoice in sufferings derives from the fact that these confirm that we are united with Christ and so we will be united with him in glory: 'Rejoice that you participate in the sufferings of Christ, so that you may be overjoyed when his glory is revealed' (4:13).

The care of the Father

In 1:6 Peter goes further. His readers 'have had to suffer'. He says that suffering is 'God's will' (3:17). God is at work *in* our sufferings and *through* our sufferings. If we remove God from our suffering, we are left with cruel, cold, impersonal suffering. But if I can recognize that my suffering is somehow and in some way coming from God himself, then my grief, though real and painful, is not relentless or futile. God's ways may be unfathomable but his character is not. We know him to be a good, wise, loving, merciful God because he has shown himself to be that by giving his Son on the cross. That one act interprets all of God's other actions, functioning as a lens through which we should view life in all of its complexity. So even when bad things happen the gospel tells us that God is at work in them for our good and his glory. 'So, then,' concludes Peter, 'those who suffer according to God's will should commit themselves to their faithful Creator and continue to do good' (4:19) just as Jesus himself did (2:23).

Peter, quoting Psalm 34, calls us to 'turn from evil and do good' knowing that 'the eyes of the Lord are on the righteous and his ears are attentive to their prayer' (3:11–12). He concludes, 'Who is going to harm you if you are eager to do good?' (3:13). The original Greek begins 'And', with the sense of 'And so, in the light of this care God shows to those who do good, who is going to harm you if you are eager to do good?' It is a promise of eternal security, not necessarily immediate protection. Peter promises that 'our gentleness and respect' will cause people to 'be ashamed of their slander' (3:16). We may look vulnerable and shamed, but we will be secure (3:13) and blessed (3:14). Our accusers look secure and blessed, but they will be judged (4:5) and shamed (3:16).

The support of the family

Peter ends his letter with a strange command, one we are often inclined to gloss over: 'Greet one another with a kiss of love' (5:14). This completes a series of calls to love one another in the Christian family (1:23; 2:1, 17; 3:8; 4:8; 5:14). Often they appear in the context of external pressure or slander (3:8–9). 'Above all, love each other deeply,' says Peter after warning that our former friends will abuse us when we refuse to join them in sin (4:8). In a world that has made us un-family, the church is our new family. It is easy for the world to ignore a solitary Christian living consistently as a believer because he or she could be dismissed as an eccentric. But if a diverse group of Christians live for Christ as a community of love and demonstrable, mutual affection, then society will find it far harder to dismiss us.

The hope of glory

There is no doubt, however, that the dominant perspective in 1 Peter that enables us to face suffering with joy is the hope of glory (1:6; 4:13).

This pattern of suffering followed by glory runs throughout the letter. Almost every paragraph contains references to suffering or submission and glory or hope. We rejoice in our hope of a future inheritance while we 'suffer grief in all kinds of trials' (1:3–6). The Scriptures point to this pattern of suffering followed by glory (1:10–12). Like Christ, Christians are rejected by men, but precious to God (2:4–8). Peter addresses elders as 'a witness of Christ's sufferings and one who also will share in the glory to be revealed', promising that they 'will receive the crown of glory that will never fade away' (5:1–4). Young men are to embrace humility so that God 'may lift you up in due time' (5:5–6). According to Eugene Boring, 1 Peter is addressed to

> those who are at the margins of society, reviled and accused . . .
> They need a larger perspective, which the author provides not in
> psychological or sociological terms of self-esteem, but by helping
> them see their privileged place in the context of God's plan for
> history, a privilege they had not achieved but had been granted by
> God's grace.[1]

Tertullian said, 'The leg does not feel the chain if the mind is in heaven.'[2]

In 3:10–17 Peter promises that for Christians suffering and slander lead to blessing and vindication. We know this because this was the experience of Christ with whom we are now united by the Spirit: 'He was put to death in the body but made alive by the Spirit' (3:18). In other words, humanity judged and rejected Jesus, but the Spirit vindicated him by raising him from the dead. Jesus 'has gone into heaven and is at God's right hand – with angels, authorities and powers in submission to him' – the ultimate vindication (3:22)!

We see the same pattern of marginalization followed by vindication in the story of Noah (3:19–21). Long ago Jesus preached through Noah, but the people of the time disobeyed his message and are now 'in prison' while Noah is saved. Noah is a natural point of reference because he is one of the supreme Old Testament examples of vindication. For years Noah built an ocean-going ship far from the sea. It is not hard to imagine the ridicule this provoked. His warnings of judgment fell on deaf ears. Perhaps, like many of us today, he had days when he wondered what he was doing. We are not told. But ultimately he was vindicated, for those who ridiculed his message were judged while Noah and his family were saved through water. Peter links this to our baptism. Whenever we remember our baptism we are reminded that we have died to this world and risen to the life of the coming age when we will be vindicated along with our Saviour.

With this pattern of slander followed by vindication established, Peter calls us to be done with sin: 'Therefore, since Christ suffered in his body, arm yourselves also with the same attitude, because he who has suffered in his body is done with sin' (4:1). The willingness to suffer is a sign of our break with sin. We do not choose to suffer per se (3:13; 4:15) but we choose to break with sin even though we know this will lead to suffering. Peter anticipates intense peer pressure when we refuse to join in doing what we used to do before our conversion:

> For you have spent enough time in the past doing what pagans choose to do – living in debauchery, lust, drunkenness, orgies, carousing and detestable idolatry. They think it strange that you do not plunge with them into the same flood of dissipation, and they heap abuse on you.
>
> (4:3–4)

But Peter's message is clear: not sinning might lead to suffering, but it is better to suffer than to sin.

We suffer 'in the body' (4:1) just as Jesus suffered 'in the body' (3:18; 4:1) knowing that we will be vindicated 'in the spirit' (4:6) just as Jesus was. Meanwhile those who abuse us will be judged (4:5). Christians 'who are now dead' appear to the world to have followed Christ in vain, but Peter says they are 'judged according to men in regard to the body, but live according to God in regard to the spirit' (4:6).

At the end of the letter Peter gives his reason for writing: 'Encouraging you and testifying that this is the true grace of God' (5:12). What is this true grace of God? The preceding verses say, 'And the God of all grace, who called you to his eternal glory in Christ, after you have suffered a little while, will himself restore you and make you strong, firm and steadfast. To him be the power for ever and ever. Amen' (5:10–11). So the true grace of God, the grace that makes God 'the God of all grace', consists of this: he has called us to eternal glory after we have suffered a little while. Suffering followed by glory.[3] Rejection followed by honour (2:4–8). Slander followed by vindication. Peter has already described Christ's suffering followed by glory as 'grace' in 1:10–11, 13 and said that suffering unjustly for Christ is commendable, literally 'a grace' (2:19).

Peter needs to write to confirm that this is 'the *true* grace of God' because there are *false* versions of grace that promise glory now or promise glory without suffering. It is a false grace of God when Christians claim our nation as Christian and expect special privileges from the state, or when Christians insist they can leave behind sickness and trials, and claim health and prosperity. It is a false grace of God when Christians leave behind the struggles and humiliations of mission and settle for the acclaim of the converted.

Peter says, 'You know that your brothers throughout the world are undergoing the same kind of sufferings' (5:9). Many of us do not currently live in an environment of active persecution. But, like Peter's readers, we live in a culture hostile to our Christian faith. To an extent we do not experience more suffering because of the historical influence of Christianity upon Western democracy. Freedom of speech remains a cherished value. Yet perhaps we also avoid persecution by our passivity. We might talk about values or ideas in the abstract, but how often do we commend Christ as our Saviour and Lord? The repeated prayer of the early church was that they might have the courage to proclaim the gospel boldly (Acts 4:29–31; Ephesians 6:19–20; Colossians 4:4–6). We too, Peter tells us, should 'not give way to fear' (3:6, 14).

Perhaps our lack of direct opposition should lead us to examine the nature and extent of our faithfulness to the Saviour? After all, Paul says, 'Everyone who wants to live a godly life in Christ Jesus will be persecuted' (2 Timothy 3:12). The relationship between godliness and suffering is not a strict quid pro quo but maybe there is an element of cause and effect. Peter calls us to set apart Christ as Lord and be done with sin (3:15; 4:1). This will lead to two responses which, though contrasting, are sometimes combined: (1) malice, slander and abuse (3:16; 4:4); and (2) questions and opportunities to talk about Jesus (3:15–16; see 2:12, 15; 3:1–2).

The challenge is this: When were you last asked to account for your hope? Are we living a life that makes no sense without the gospel? If we live out our relationship with Christ in a way that expresses itself in distinctive obedience to his lordship then the world will either be drawn to that light or try to extinguish it.

Resourcing everyday church

By definition a church on the margins will not have access to the resources of the mainstream. So how can we live well on the margins and how can we resource such an act of perpetual revolution? Most of the time it comes down to how we answer such mundane questions as: How can we do missional church when life is busy? How can we combine everyday mission with a full-time job? How can we find leaders when we are seeking to multiply groups across a city? And how are we to be funded?

Peter's call to follow the way of the cross and embrace the pattern of suffering followed by glory provides the essential framework in which we must approach these issues. Once again it is hope that changes everything. Whether it is money, career or the pressures of leadership, it is our 'living hope' that is to determine our priorities. We thrive on the margins because we are men and women of the gospel with eternity burning in our hearts.

1. Material generosity: money in eternal perspective
There is a sense in which sin is contextual. One generation's temptations are different from those of a previous generation.

This is part of the way in which 'your enemy the devil prowls around like a roaring lion looking for someone to devour' (5:8). We need to be alert because the devil changes his point of attack. Not many Christians living in central London today struggle with the temptation to bow before an image of Viracocha, the Inca god of creation. But idolatry is alive and well around St James's Park even if it is not carved out of wood. We need to take a stand precisely in those areas in our culture where sin is at its most rampant.

One such area is our attitude to possessions. It hardly needs saying that we live in a materialistic culture. Many believe the material world is all that exists, and most believe it is all that matters. We treasure 'things' that can be touched. Not only do they provide pleasure, but they also give identity. This is how we make our mark in the world. Much of contemporary Western life is given over to the pursuit of possessions or security in wealth. Part of the explanation for this cultural obsession is the complete loss of any sense of eternity. If this life is all there is then the acquisition of more here and now makes sense.

But the gospel makes a contradictory claim. Christians are a people of the future, the future that Christ has secured for us: 'In his great mercy [God the Father] has given us new birth into a living hope through the resurrection of Jesus Christ from the dead' (1:3). This does not mean that life here and now is irrelevant but that this life is to be lived in the light of eternity.

Jesus captures this perspective in his call not to 'store up for yourselves treasures on earth, where moth and rust destroy, and where thieves break in and steal. But store up for yourselves treasures in heaven, where moth and rust do not destroy, and where thieves do not break in and steal' (Matthew 6:19–20). Or again in this one-verse parable: 'The kingdom of heaven is like treasure hidden in a field. When a man found it, he hid it again, and then in his joy went and sold all he had and bought that field' (Matthew 13:44). Adverts promise meaning, identity and fulfilment through possessions. But Jesus says true treasure is found in him. He also says, 'Where your treasure is, there your heart will be also' (Matthew 6:21). Your bank statement will reveal what really matters to you. Your credit card receipts reveal who you truly serve.

Paul says that God 'richly provides us with everything for our enjoyment' (1 Timothy 6:17). But then he addresses those who are rich, which in our world, where over a billion people live on less than a dollar a day, includes you! Echoing Jesus, Paul says, 'Command them to do good, to be rich in good deeds, and to be generous and willing to share. In this way they will lay up treasure for themselves as a firm foundation for the coming age, so that they may take hold of the life that is truly life' (1 Timothy 6:18–19). Be rich therefore not in terms of wealth, but in good deeds. John Rockefeller was one of the richest men in history. After his death someone asked his accountant: 'How much money did he leave?' The accountant answered, 'All of it!'

So the goodness of creation means that wealth is good and to be received with thankfulness. But the coming new creation relativizes the claims of wealth and liberates us to use it to bless others. John Calvin reflects this perspective when he condemns 'ostentatious banquets, bodily apparel and domestic architecture' – what we would describe today as fancy dinner parties, the latest fashions and home improvements. He writes:

All these things are defended under the pretext of Christian freedom. They say that these are things indifferent. I admit it, provided they are used indifferently. But when they are coveted too greedily, when they are proudly boasted of, when they are lavishly squandered, things that were of themselves otherwise lawful are certainly defiled by these vices.

Wealth and possessions, says Calvin, are

good creations of God, permitted, indeed appointed, for men's use by God's providence. And we have never been forbidden to laugh, or to be filled, or to join new possessions to old or ancestral ones, or to delight in musical harmony, or to drink wine.

But we can also 'intoxicate mind and heart with present pleasures and be always panting after new ones – such are very far removed from a lawful use of God's gifts'.[4]

If someone moves to a new area we may commend a local church to them as a 'good church'. But what criteria do we use to make such an assessment? Preaching? Youth work? Music? For Peter a good church is characterized by love, compassion, forgiveness, generosity, service and grace (4:7–11). The preaching may be eloquent and biblical, but if that is the primary characteristic then the church is merely a good preaching centre. The music may be stirring and skilled, but if that is the primary characteristic then the church is merely a good worship centre. A good church is one where the believers share their lives together as an alternative and authentic society. Such a church will be well resourced because no-one holds what they have or who they are with a clenched fist. Just as a flower unfolds before the warmth and light of the sun, so our hands open as they are exposed to the grace of God in Christ. Grace produces grace, which is why a gospel community can only be a community of open-handed, undeserved generosity.

A 'good' church is therefore a church in which the people 'offer hospitality' – not merely as a duty, but 'without grumbling' (4:9). Cheerful hospitality will only take place when we are convinced that nothing we have is our own but that everything we have has been given to us so that others might be blessed. That is the point Peter makes in 4:10: 'Each one should use whatever gift he has received to serve others, faithfully administering God's grace in its various forms.' Believers are the God-given means of grace to one another as we love one another deeply, serve one another sacrificially and honour one another humbly.

The key idea in 4:10 is that we are stewards or administrators who faithfully 'administer' God's grace. That is a radical concept. If I am a steward then I own nothing. Everything I have is a gift and it has been given to me to be a means of God blessing others. Consider the community created by the gospel through the Holy Spirit in the aftermath of Pentecost. We are told that, 'All the believers were one in heart and mind. No-one claimed that any of his possessions was his own, but they shared everything they had' (Acts 4:32). This is the biblical doctrine of stewardship.

Jeff Vanderstelt of Soma Communities, Tacoma, USA encourages their gospel communities to write down on a large sheet of paper all the ways in which God has blessed them: their skills, time and possessions (from houses down to socks). The impossibility of the task is part of its message. Once they have filled the paper, he asks, 'Why has God blessed us with these things?' The answer, of course, is so that we might be a blessing to others in a way that brings him glory. The church does not lack resources, not when Christians view their possessions in the light of eternity.

I, Tim, think of my own gospel community. There is a lovely freedom from possessions: DVDs, books, tools and cars are all freely shared without hesitation. Time is likewise held lightly so people are quick to help with repairs, gardens, chores and childcare. Not only is hospitality common, but people routinely bake extra food and take it round for others to enjoy. I often find that cakes have mysteriously appeared in our kitchen. I know from my visits to other churches that this is common. Such attitudes can never be promulgated through legalism. This is a lifestyle that defies explanation apart from the liberating impact of the gospel. And it is this that gives missional power to these acts.

Such an attitude to material things is both appealing and disconcerting to unbelievers, both invitation and threat. This is one way in which our churches are communities of both grace and judgment. The world is forced to respond. People may be attracted by this hope-filled lifestyle and begin to enquire about the reason for our hope (3:15). Or they may be repelled by a lifestyle that exposes the emptiness of their materialism.

2. Relational generosity: time in eternal perspective

'Love covers over a multitude of sins,' says Peter (4:8). A key aspect of the marginalized Christian community must be its capacity for forgiveness or what we might call 'relational generosity'.

There is an idea that being in community means that we have the freedom to tell someone if they have offended us in any way. But Peter says that our primary responsibility is to love one another. That means that when someone hurts us we are not required to confront them. Why? Because love has covered it. Love does not minimize wrongdoing; it covers it, deals with it and even in a sense pays for it. There are two popular ways that we deal with offence. I can confront the person to 'get it off my chest'. Or I can hide it away in my consciousness and emotionally distance myself from the offender. Neither of these responses is appropriate. You love them with a love strong, deep, passionate and gracious enough to cover their sin.

People often ask how Christian community looks different from the kind of friendship enjoyed by others. The answer comes at the point of tension. Every community experiences relational tension. That is a fact of life. But in a Spirit-filled, gospel community that tension leads to the glory of God: 'Love each other deeply, because love covers over a multitude of sins . . . so that in all things God may be praised through Jesus Christ' (1 Peter 4:8, 11).

'If anyone speaks, he should do it as one speaking the very words of God. If anyone serves, he should do it with the strength God provides' (4:11). Most commentators assume that this speaking and serving refer to the formal roles of preachers and deacons. But Peter is addressing everyone as members of this new society. He is telling us all to talk with a certain sense of 'weightiness'. Our words should build others up, bring the gospel to bear and speak of Christ. Servant-heartedness is to characterize not only leaders but the whole church. The apostle is passionate about gospel living for everyone in the everyday. His focus is not so-called professionals or the super-talented, but ordinary people living together by grace.

Living in missional community requires not only forgiveness but time. Relationships are time-intensive. Everyday church fills every day. But it does not necessarily fill it with extra activities. It is about living ordinary life with gospel intentionality, doing what we already do with other people and with a commitment to speak of Jesus, whether to encourage believers or evangelize unbelievers. This is what a member of my gospel community wrote in an email:

I have felt working full-time that I don't have much time to do the thing I love most which is spending time with people. I get home from work, eat some dinner, give my wife a kiss and then I only have two hours until bed and I am usually feeling tired. The easy thing to do is watch television, talk with my wife and then go to bed!

I've had to learn that I *do* have time. We've decided we need to include people more and more into the mundane, everyday tasks that we do so we spend more time with our church and community. What that could look like is having people over for an ordinary dinner and let beans on toast be enough! Or taking the dog for a walk past a friend's house and stopping in for a cup of tea. Or, instead of watching television on our own, have others come hang out and watch it together. I was forgetting that this is what we are all about: just hanging out, doing nothing spectacular, but with gospel intentionality.

But still many people struggle to find time even to share life with others because their life is their work. If possessions can be a means of identity, so too can careers. In Western culture one of the first questions we ask when we first meet someone is, 'What do you do for a living?' We answer the question 'Who are you?' with a job title.

Christians have every reason to value work. God himself is a worker. He has given us his creation to explore, maintain, order and develop, and with it a mandate for technology, art, culture, science, industry and commerce. We are called to glorify God and bless others through work. But work is not our core identity.

Imagine a follower of Christ who is very able at her work, a rising star, not only in her company, but in her profession. Imagine that woman choosing to maintain a forty-hour week in which she is diligent and committed, but refusing to work extra hours because of her commitment to her gospel community. How would her colleagues view her? How would her employers treat her? Extend that principle to a local church made up of people from various walks of life who have not been seduced by the accolades society gives to those who 'sell their soul to the company'. We might find people who have chosen part-time work so they can help out in a local drugs project. Or people who have left a promising career so they can serve the disadvantaged. We might also find people who have continued to climb the corporate ladder, but without compromising their integrity, giving them unique opportunities to witness to Christ.

Such choices are possible because of eternity. In fact, such choices make sense *only* in the light of our eternal hope. This eternal perspective means that even if we should lose our job or be overlooked for promotion or abandoned by our boss, we live as those with hope and so commend Christ.[5]

In the end it comes back to identity. We build our lives around how we see ourselves. If you see yourself first and foremost as a businessman or housewife or a professional then you will build your life around this with church as part of an orbiting fringe of activities. But if you see yourself first and foremost as a member of God's missional people then you will build your life around this identity. Jobs, house, incomes are made to fit round your core identity.

Not only do you build your life around the community, but the community builds its life around you as a member of that community. So, for example, if together you decide that your work is your primary ministry then others will support that pursuit. We have someone in our missional communities who has started an engineering business. At each stage of its development he has involved the community in his decision-making. He has a strong vision for blessing others through his products and generating income for the kingdom of God.

Starting a new business is demanding. But being part of a Christian community is not one-way traffic. The community shares his vision and supports his work. When his wife was unwell, people provided meals and childcare over a period of several months. His business is not just his ministry, it is *our* ministry.

3. Leadership: pressure in eternal perspective

Leadership is vital and necessary. Every group will have leaders, whether you appointed them or not. Someone will emerge who shapes the culture. So it is important to ensure you have in place leaders with the character described in 1 Timothy 3 and Titus 1, leaders who can set a gospel culture through their leadership, teaching and example. To lead a gospel community you do not necessarily need to be able to deliver a forty-minute sermon but you do need to be able to apply the gospel faithfully to people's lives. What counts most is not charisma or eloquence but godly character.

Leadership is vital and necessary in the context of a marginalized church. This is why Peter turns from talking about suffering to the subject of leadership in 5:1–4. He begins his appeal to leaders: 'So . . .' (5:1 ESV), thereby highlighting this connection. And he returns to the theme of suffering in 5:6–11. Moreover he makes his appeal as 'a witness of Christ's sufferings'. Leaders have a crucial role to play when believers are under pressure. Shepherds are needed because the flock is harassed and in danger of being scattered. And once again it is hope that is to shape the attitude of leaders: 'Be shepherds of God's flock . . . And when the Chief Shepherd appears, you will receive the crown of glory that will never fade away' (1 Peter 5:2, 4). How does this work out in practice?

Willingness rather than obligation. 'Be shepherds of God's

flock that is under your care,' says Peter, 'serving as over-
seers – not because you must, but because you are willing, as
God wants you to be' (5:2). There was a time when a young
man had various career options open to him, one of which
included 'going into the church'. Although a clerical position
may not have offered the most attractive remuneration, it
came with a number of perks, not least impressive housing
and social status. That would not have been the case among
the churches to which Peter was writing and it is never the
situation when the church is marginalized. Edmund Clowney
observes,

> In some American and British churches Peter's exhortation
> would seem strange. Why should any elder serve unwillingly? The
> responsibility of church office has been trivialized; it is no more than
> a minor inconvenience that can readily be declined. But in countries
> where conversion to Christ is illegal and baptism brings a prison
> sentence, the office of the elder carries a different meaning. Quite
> apart from persecution, any real shepherd of Christ's flock will soon
> feel the weight of pastoral care.[6]

Enthusiasm rather than greed. Peter calls for leaders who are
'not greedy for money, but eager to serve' (5:2). We cannot
fill our cities with communities of light if every gospel community must be led by a salaried leader who has studied at
a residential Bible college. We need to raise up an army of
leaders who like Paul earn money during the day and serve
in the church in the evening (1 Thessalonians 2:9), leaders
whose life choices are not determined by salaries and pen-
sions, but who take risks for the gospel and model reliance
on God. Authentic leadership can be bi-vocational and in
a marginalized context this may be preferable. Unbelievers
are often suspicious of 'professional clergy'. They are more

willing to listen to someone who works hard with integrity in a 'normal' job. This also brings leaders into contact with people who would never attend a church service.

Example rather than diktat. Bi-vocational leadership also enables leaders to model what it means to live credibly in a context of suspicion and animosity. Peter says that leaders should serve, 'not lording it over those entrusted to you, but being examples to the flock' (5:3). The story is told of a guide showing a group of tourists around the countryside outside Jerusalem. He had told them how a shepherd always leads the sheep from the front and never drives them from behind. As the bus was taking them back into the city, a tourist pointed out a flock of sheep being driven from behind by a man shouting and waving a stick. 'I thought you said a shepherd would never do that?' protested the disappointed tourist. The guide stopped the bus to find out what was happening. He came back with a smile on his face. 'That's not the shepherd. It's the butcher!' he said. Peter calls elders to lead from the front, to lead by example rather than driving from behind by command. Leaders should lead the way in mission. Yet in many churches leaders have fewer unbelieving friends than most people in the congregation. Leadership is not so much about developing a programme that others follow as creating a culture in which others flourish.

Whether it is money, time or leadership the key is hope, just as it was with our attitude to suffering. It is those who lay up treasure in heaven who are generous with the treasures of earth. It is those who live for eternity that are free to give time to mission. It is leaders who live for 'the crown of glory that will never fade away' (5:4) who serve willingly and eagerly (5:2).

4. Prayer as a missionary activity

How will we resource missional communities? Resources will come from a Christian community shaped by hope. But our ultimate resource is God himself. Peter concludes: 'The God of all grace, who called you to his eternal glory in Christ, after you have suffered a little while, will himself restore you and make you strong, firm and steadfast' (5:10). God himself supplies what we need. 'Cast all your anxiety on him,' says Peter, 'because he cares for you' (5:7). So prayer needs to be central to our mission strategy. Peter says, 'The end of all things is near. Therefore be clear minded and self-controlled so that you can pray' (4:7).

This is a truth we all know in our heads, but our practice so often reflects an assumption that our actions are what matter. So why do we not make prayer central? Perhaps because we think mission depends on us or because we want to be in control. If we think we are central to gospel growth then our activity will always seem more urgent than prayer. During a season in which some of us met for prayer at 9am three mornings a week, I would find myself back at my desk at 10.30 thinking, 'Half the morning has gone and I've not done anything!' It revealed the extent to which I think my activity is what matters rather than God's. If we want to be in control then we will restrict ourselves to situations in which we are comfortable. If my strategy is to persuade people with carefully constructed arguments then I am in control (and if I am not then I read a book to acquire better arguments). But if I pray with an unbeliever for a specific need then I am not in control of the outcome. Yet this scary reliance on God is precisely what we want to cultivate. This is a strategy that lets God be the primary agent of mission; that lets God be God. 'If anyone speaks,' says Peter, 'he should do it as one speaking the very words of God. If anyone serves, he should do it with the strength God provides, so that in all things God may be praised through Jesus Christ' (4:11). Peter echoes the sentiment of Paul: 'My message and my preaching were not with wise and persuasive words, but with a demonstration of the Spirit's power, so that your faith might not rest on men's wisdom, but on God's power' (1 Corinthians 2:4–5), and 'We have this treasure in jars of clay to show that this all-surpassing power is from God and not from us' (2 Corinthians 4:7).

So we need to view prayer as a missional activity. For us this involves three things. First, it involves routine, regular, organized prayer. In other words, we arrange to pray together because this is our primary missional activity. Secondly, it involves a reflex towards impromptu prayer. In other words, we try to make it common to pray whenever and wherever and with whomever, as needs arise. Thirdly, we offer prayer as a service to unbelievers. So when unbelievers talk of problems, we say things such as 'Would you like me to pray with you?' or 'I'll ask my church to pray about that.' This allows us to ask people follow-up questions, such as 'We've been praying for you. What's the news?' This not only shows love for people, but it also demonstrates that we have a living relationship with God and that he is not simply an idea to be debated and about which we have opinions. We heard, for example, that the son of a couple from a Muslim background was having nightmares. So someone promised that we would pray for him, which we did. A few days later they told us the nightmares had stopped. This created a conversation about the kindness and power of Jesus.

So we want to make prayer our first recourse when needs or opportunities arise. Prayer is not a support activity to mission. It is itself a frontline activity. Mission is never under our control. It is God who is the great missionary.

Questions for gospel communities

Here are some questions to help us apply the above. You can
do this exercise on your own, by asking whether the statements below are true of you as an individual and of your
gospel community. Or you can do this exercise with a group,
by asking them to identify those statements that are clearly
true of your community and those which are clearly untrue.
Celebrate what God is doing among you and identify what
you could do better.

A. God: Are you God-centred?

1. People often extol the goodness and greatness of God in
   normal conversation.
2. Our corporate worship stirs people's affections for God
   (their love, fear, hope, confidence, desire).
3. Prayer is a regular part of our life together.
4. People pray together outside meetings, as and when
   issues arise.
5. When we pray as a community most people contribute
   and . . .
6. When we pray as a community it is sometimes difficult
   because people readily contribute.
7. Our prayer requests focus on God and his glory rather
   than on us and our comfort.
8. We are trusting in God's sovereignty rather than trying
   to do his work of conversion or worrying about
   'results'.

B. Love: Are you other-centred?

1. People often see one another between scheduled
   meetings.
2. Most people eat with other members of the community
   at least twice a week.

3. People often help in practical ways like doing chores for one another.
4. People feel a sense of responsibility for one another.
5. People use the language of 'we' rather than 'you': 'We should . . .' rather than 'You should . . .'
6. People are generous with their time, money, homes and possessions.
7. People are willing to discuss their time and money.
8. People make decisions with regard to the community and in consultation with the community.

C. The Bible: Are you Word-centred?

1. There is a hunger for God's Word and an excitement when it is taught.
2. People often talk about how the Holy Spirit is speaking to them through his Word.
3. The Word of God is often discussed outside scheduled Bible studies.
4. People meet up to read the Bible together.
5. There is evidence that the Word is changing individual lives.
6. There is evidence that the Word is changing the life of the community as a whole.
7. People speak the truth in love when others face pastoral issues.
8. People look to the truth about God rather than blaming their circumstances.

D. Grace: Are you grace-centred?

1. People are open about their sin and struggles rather than hiding or pretending.
2. Conflict is open rather than suppressed and reconciliation is proactively pursued.

3. People repent of sinful attitudes such as anxiety, pride, complaining, fear of others, self-justification, bitterness, anger and selfishness.
4. People repent of good works done for self-righteous motives.
5. People are not afraid to make mistakes.
6. People feel able to relax and enjoy leisure activities.
7. Broken people are attracted to our community.
8. We constantly return to the cross in our conversation, prayers and praise.

E. Mission: Are you mission-centred?

1. Unbelievers are involved in the life of our community.
2. We often have opportunities to talk about Jesus.
3. We are flexible and take risks for the sake of the gospel.
4. We are crossing cultural boundaries.
5. We are blessing our neighbourhood and city.
6. We value involvement in work, business, art, culture, public service and government.
7. We have a vision to start a new gospel community or congregation.
8. We are actively and generously involved in mission around the world.

CONCLUSION: THE NEXT STEPS

Christians today are marginalized, slandered and mocked. But as we have seen, the churches to which Peter wrote faced a similar situation. Peter does not offer sympathy. He does not say, 'I'm sorry to hear you're in a difficult situation. I hope you can make the best of it.' Nor does he treat it as abnormal. He does not say, 'I can't believe the way people talk about the Christian faith. It's outrageous. We need a campaign.' The people of God have always experienced hostility. Jesus himself was marginalized and faced ultimate rejection on the cross. This is the One whom we follow.

But, despite our marginalization, Peter remains confident that we have something to offer our culture. We can still make an impact. Just as Jesus is the stone 'rejected by men' whom God has made the capstone (2:7), so rejected Christians are 'a chosen people, a royal priesthood, a holy nation, a people belonging to God' (2:9). This is who you are, says Peter. Not nobodies, not no-good neighbours that everybody despises, but a chosen people, a royal priesthood, a holy nation.

Reading 1 Peter we get intoxicated with the idea of church again and again. It is almost as though the smell of what it means to be the people of God emanates from the letter. It is mind-blowing and heart-stirring. We love the concept of the church!

Let's imagine

Yet we have been around long enough to know that the reality rarely matches the rhetoric. Maybe you even find yourself asking, 'Are we always going to have to settle for mediocrity?' So we have a few questions:

- Do we have the imagination to be what we can and should be as the people of God?
- Do we have the desire to be the people of God together on mission?
- Can we move beyond church as a weekly service and become a community who share life and share mission?
- Can we be a people for whom church and mission are our identity rather than occasional events?

We think this is achievable. It may never perfectly match the biblical ideal because the church is made up of people who, though saved by grace, continue to struggle with sin. The church is not ideal because I am not ideal. But some approximation is possible. Let's be clear, God does not call us to mediocrity, nor does he call us to be a community on mission and then mock our failures. He gave his Son and sends his

Spirit so that we can be his people and live as his people. We should be able to take the reality of church life, place a biblical vision of church alongside it and say, 'Yes, I can see the resemblance. There may not be an exact fit, but they are recognizably similar.'

So how can we put a vision for everyday church and everyday mission into practice?

We are often asked about how we do things within The Crowded House. We are normally reluctant to respond. We do not want to put ourselves forward as the answer. While we love our church and count it a huge privilege to be part of it, we are well aware of its failings too. Nor do we have a structure that we regard as some kind of blueprint for others. We often find people attributing a model to us, often wrongly. But we do not advocate a model of church. Instead we advocate principles that need to be adapted to each context. In fact, there are different structures within the wider The Crowded House family of churches and we ourselves have often adjusted our pattern over the years.

But let us describe how we organize church life at the moment in The Crowded House Sheffield where we both serve as elders. We do so simply to encourage people to think creatively about how they might organize church life for everyday church and mission. Let this stimulate your imagination but forget the blueprint idea.

Also everyday church is not primarily about a structure but about a culture or ethos. You cannot organize people to do everyday church through structures and programmes. People need to catch a vision and learn how to live that out day by day. Structures can help or hinder, but they cannot generate a communal identity or a missional lifestyle. Primarily everyday church needs to be taught and modelled.

A gathering of gospel communities

Currently we have a number of gospel communities scattered across the city. They are the heart of church life, church at street level. This is where community, mission, pastoral care, prayer, baptism, Communion and the application of God's Word take place.

Once a week the gospel communities come together for what we call a 'gathering'. The gospel communities are the primary focus for church life, but the gathering is also an expression of church. It represents the people of God assembled together under the Word of God. So, although the primary place of belonging is the gospel community, the weekly event is also important. This is where we stir our minds and our hearts to action through singing God's praises together, sharing stories to inspire one another and learning from the Word. For us this is where the main Bible teaching normally takes place. Here we set the vision and culture for our gospel communities. This allows gospel communities to focus their energies on community and mission. They are also encouraged to apply what has been taught in the gathering to the specifics of their lives and their life together.

But our gathering is just a couple of hours a week. It is in our gospel communities that church happens day by day. This is the context in which we are in and out of one another's lives and homes, sharing meals, resources, problems, joys, sorrows and opportunities. Sharing life. In our gospel communities we are being the people of God together on mission. So we describe our gospel communities as churches and speak of our gathering as a gathering *of* gospel communities rather than a gathering *with* gospel communities.

In any context the weekly gathering is going to be important for setting a gospel culture and a missional vision. But it cannot achieve all that the New Testament envisions for church life. For example, it cannot be a context for the 'one anothering' of the New Testament. Moreover if it is seen as primary then all these other things are viewed as secondary. If the bulk of a church's time and energy goes into the Sunday meeting then everyday church will not happen.

Doing church as a large gathering is the easy option. You can be friends with anyone when you just meet for a couple of hours on a Sunday morning and spend most of that time singing and listening to someone else talking. But in a gospel community you are forced to rub shoulders with people day by day. People let you down and disappoint you. People say things about you or do not do things they said they would do. That is when it is hard to love and serve and forgive. But it is precisely in the everyday that we are called to be the people of God. If we are not the people of God in these moments then we cannot claim to be the people of God on a Sunday morning.

We often find ourselves accused of being against big church. It is not true. We do not care what size your gathering is. Our focus is not on what happens on a Sunday morning. Our cutting edge is gospel communities living lives together on mission out there at street level. What we do in our gathering is designed to facilitate and sharpen that everyday life of the church. So it is wrong to say we do not like big church. What we do not like are big events that distract from the everyday, pull resources away from the everyday and switch the focus from everyday church to a weekly performance.

We also often find ourselves accused of being against monologue preaching. Again, this is not true. Our gatherings typically involve a sermon. What we question is the privileged status of the monologue. It is a good way to teach the Bible but it is not the only way nor a necessary way. The Bible itself describes the Word being taught through a variety of methods without privileging one above another. What matters is that the Word is central to our lives and our life together. We want to equip and liberate people to proclaim the Bible to one another throughout the week. We want the Word pushed down into everyday life.

The gospel community is an identity, a community of God's people doing mission together. The gathering, too, is more than a meeting. It is the network of gospel communities working together to reach the city. The gathering of gospel communities has a shared leadership which better enables us to cooperate. It also means we can put younger leaders in place within a supportive structure and create gospel communities on the fly in response to evangelistic opportunities. This collective identity with a collective meeting means that the church is more reproducible. We do not need a lot in place to start a new gospel community because leaders are supported by a wider network, and good Bible teaching is assured through the gathering. So gospel communities can be light, flexible and adaptable. They can even be expendable in the sense that we can innovate and take risks without fear of failure.

Gospel communities can also be encouraged to adapt their activities, location, style and so on to suit the people they are trying to reach. They are free to be very contextual expressions of church, perhaps with a focus on a specific ethnic or social group because the gathering gives full expression to the unity we have in Christ that transcends cultural differences. We want to express both the particularity of the gospel (through contextual gospel communities) and the universality of the gospel (through the unity of the gathering).

Transitioning to everyday church

So how can you transition a church to one where the focus is on everyday church and mission?

If you are a large church then our advice is not to change all your structures but to create a working model. In other words, say to a handful of people, 'Go, do it.' Teach them, train them, lead them, show them and then release them to be a gospel community within your church. Then encourage this group to talk to other people about how it is going: their vision, joys and frustrations. In this way people have the chance to observe a gospel community in action. Then, as you teach about how the gospel gives us a communal and missional identity, you can point to what is happening and say this is what it looks like. As people hear what is happening it may spark their imagination and they too may start to catch the vision.

You may then want to take your home groups or small groups and release them to be gospel communities. Give them a mandate to be church and to do mission and reproduce. Rather than dismantle church life you can gradually shift the focus to everyday church. Make the gospel communities the front door and the gathering the support structure, rather than the other way round. Or keep a big lighthouse model of church with its beam of light sweeping across the whole city, but at the same time get that light dispersed at street level through the gospel communities.

If you are a small church then be a gospel community. Stop worrying about putting on events and programmes that mirror big churches. Instead start being the people of God together on mission. Hang out together throughout the week. Get in and out of one another's homes. Let people know the struggles you are facing and the opportunities you enjoy. Find ways in which your lives can intersect with one another. Invite unbelievers to be part of this community life.

When I, Steve, first started doing gospel community we acted as though we were a big church. We tried to compress a large gathering into someone's front room. It was embarrassing. I even spoke from a lectern. With a small gathering you have the opportunity to be relaxed, informal, just to be God's people together without any paraphernalia. When you outgrow a front room you can think about creating two gospel communities and perhaps coming together in a slightly larger venue on a regular basis.

What stops you doing everyday church?
Below are five obstacles that encourage people to maintain existing structures even when they prevent us from being the people of God together on mission.

1. The first obstacle is one we touched on in chapter 2: the endemic individualism of our culture that also pervades our attitudes as Christians. Our culture has made a virtue of an integral part of our fallenness: our desire to control our own lives. This is the air we breathe. I assume the right to live my life as if it is all about me and make decisions for myself without reference to others.

2. A second obstacle is pride. We prize self-sufficiency. 'I did it on my own,' we say, not with shame, but with pride. 'I did it my way.' But the biblical picture of church says we need to live in community because the Christian life is a communal life. I need you and you need me.

3. A third obstacle is our desire for comfort. We do not want to open our lives and homes to others. People we like are OK, but everyday church puts all sorts of people in our path and on our sofa. We do not like to move out of our comfort zones.

4. Fear is the fourth obstacle, the fear that people might see me for who I really am, up close and personal. I can

appear a great Christian in the pulpit or in the pew each Sunday. But I cannot appear a great Christian when people see me lose my temper with my children or answer my wife sharply.

5. Obstacle number five is people. Libraries, they say, would be wonderful places to run if it were not for people wanting to borrow books. Many people have the same attitude towards missional church. They are inspired by the theory of community and mission. They read all the books and endlessly lecture their friends. They love the church in the abstract. And so they are dismissive of actual churches, none of which matches their ideals. If only there was a way to do community without people! People, it is true, *are* a problem. When you start sharing everyday life then you see one another's issues. But my brothers and sisters are *my* problem just as *I* am theirs. And just as I am to be a means of grace to them, so they will be a means of grace to me.

So what are the solutions? The first is the gospel. The people of God living life together on mission *is the good life*, life as it was meant to be lived. We see this in creation: we are made for community with God and others, and to reflect God's glory in his world. We see this in Abraham and Israel: at the heart of God's purposes are not isolated individuals, but a people whose life is to draw the nations to God. We see this in Jesus: the true Israel, the true people of God and the light of the world who calls his disciples to be his new community, a city on a hill that cannot be hidden. We see this in the new creation: God dwells among his people and makes them his own. God's purpose has always been to have a people who are his people and through whom he reveals his glory in the world. This is how God defines the good life: the people of God together in community making known the glory of God. Jesus did not die to save isolated individuals but for his church. He died and rose and sent the Spirit to create a people who would be his people and through whom he would reveal his glory. And because it is the gospel it has to be solution number one and there is no solution number two. If you want to keep a professional view of church with a life detached from other believers, you do not understand the gospel.

Everyday church will expose our idols. You never really know what drives you until you live in community. Other people threaten or thwart our sinful desires. Suddenly our idols keep popping up all over the place. They sit comfortably on the mantelpiece of our heart until somebody knocks them off. Then we cry out in protest or dive to catch them. But let them fall! Yet the pain of having our idols smashed only serves to point us to the one true Lord.

Everyday church will either witness to God's grace in our lives or it will fracture. We cannot 'achieve' it, for it grows out of God's grace to us and to others. It is the fruit of grace and therefore a testimony to grace. When people see us living life together, loving, serving, forgiving, forbearing, supporting, encouraging and proclaiming the gospel to one another, it cannot but provoke questions.

> Finally, all of you, live in harmony with one another; be sympathetic, love as brothers, be compassionate and humble . . . In your hearts set apart Christ as Lord. Always be prepared to give an answer to everyone who asks you to give the reason for the hope that you have. But do this with gentleness and respect.
>
> (1 Peter 3:8, 15)

NOTES

Introduction

1. Tim Chester and Steve Timmis, *Total Church: A Radical Reshaping Around Gospel and Community* (IVP/Crossway, 2007/2009).

1. Life at the margins

1. See Jacinta Ashworth and Ian Farthing, 'Churchgoing in the UK' (Tearfund, 2007). The Tearfund Report and the UK Government's British Social Attitudes surveys asked about 'typical' church attendance across the UK and produced figures of 10% and 9.5% respectively.

2. The English Church Census is based on a snapshot of a particular week, and it suggests that 6.1% of the population of England attend church. Evangelical Alliance UK, '2005 Church Census' (www. eauk.org/resources/info/statistics/2005englishchurchcensus.cfm), November 2006.

3. Evangelical Alliance UK, '2005 Church Census' (www.eauk.org/resources/info/statistics/2005englishchurchcensus.cfm), November 2006.

4. Maria Mackay, 'Researcher Anticipates Further Church Decline in 2010s', *Christian Today* (www.christiantoday.com/article/researcher. anticipates.further.church.decline.in.2010s/25949.htm), 22 May 2010.

5. Philip Richter and Leslie Francis, *Gone But Not Forgotten* (DLT, 1998).

6. *Mission-Shaped Church: Church Planting and Fresh Expressions of Church in a Changing Context* (Church House Publishing, 2004), pp. 36–39.

7. Jacinta Ashworth and Ian Farthing, 'Churchgoing in the UK' (Tearfund, 2007), pp. 7, 24. This report found that a third of UK adults are de-churched and a third are non-churched, but these proportions exclude adherents of other religions. The report found that 15% of UK adults attend church at least once a month, with a further 10% fringe who attend at least once a year. Of the remaining 75%, 6% claim they might attend at some point in the future. This leaves almost 70% with no intention of ever attending a church service.

8. Ibid., p. 25.

9. Ibid., p. 18.

10. Jim Petersen, *Church Without Walls: Moving Beyond Traditional Boundaries* (NavPress, 1992), pp. 110–111.

11. Cited in Greater Europe Mission, 'European Christian Demographics' (www.joshuaproject.net/assets/unreachedeurope. pdf). The least responsive mega-peoples are Swedish, Russian, Lithuanian, Polish, Georgian, Serb, French, Irish, Czech and Italian.

12. Greater Europe Mission, 'European Christian Demographics' (www.joshuaproject.net/assets/unreachedeurope.pdf).

13. John Bellamy and Keith Castle, *2001 Church Attendance Estimates* (National Church Life Survey, Occasional Paper 3, 2004), p. 11 and *Operation World*.

14. Ruth Powell and Kathy Jacka, *Moving Beyond Forty Years of Missing Generations* (National Church Life Survey, Occasional Paper 10, 2008), p. 6.

15. Rob Spink, 'Work Culture', spinkingoutloud.wordpress.com, 25 July 2010 (spinkingoutloud.wordpress.com/2010/07/25/work-culture).

16. The Barna Group, 'New Statistics on Church Attendance and Avoidance', barna.org, 3 March 2008 (www.barna.org/barna-update/article/18-congregations/45-new-statistics-on-church-attendance-and-avoidance).

17. The statistical picture is muddied by differing definitions and methodologies. Americans often use 'un-churched' to refer to people who do not attend church regularly rather than people who never have any contact with a church.

18. According to the Barna research, 42% of people in the North-West are un-churched (or de-churched) and 39% in the North-East.

19. The Barna Group, 'New Statistics on Church Attendance and Avoidance', barna.org, 3 March 2008 (www.barna.org/barna-update/article/18-congregations/45-new-statistics-on-church-attendance-and-avoidance).

20. The Barna Group, 'Un-churched Population Nears 100 Million in the U.S.', barna.org, 19 March 2007 (www.barna.org/barna-update/article/12-faithspirituality/107-un-churched-population-nears-100-million-in-the-us).

21. Scott Thomas, 'This Is Why We Plant Churches', Mars Hill Blog, 21 October 2010 (blog.marshillchurch.org/2010/10/21/this-is-why-we-plant-churches) and D. J. Chuang, 'Churches Closing and Pastors Leaving', djchuang.com, 31 January 2010 (djchuang.com/2010/churches-closing-and-pastors-leaving).

22. Cited in Eddie Gibbs, *Church Next: Quantum Changes in Christian Ministry* (IVP, 2000), p. 15.

23. Peter Berger, 'Secularization Falsified', *First Things* (February 2008) (www.firstthings.com/article/2008/01/002-secularization-falsified-1);

see also Peter Berger, Effie Fokas and Grace Davie, *Religious America, Secular Europe?* (Ashgate, 2008).

24. Peter Berger, 'Secularization Falsified', *First Things* (February 2008) (www.firstthings.com/article/2008/01/002-secularization-falsified-1); see also Peter Berger, Effie Fokas and Grace Davie, *Religious America, Secular Europe?* (Ashgate, 2008).

25. George G. Hunter, *How to Reach Secular People* (Abingdon, 1992), p. 24.

26. Lyndon Bowring, 'At the Heart of CARE', *CARE Today* 20 (Autumn 2010), p. 4.

27. Stuart Murray, *Post-Christendom: Church and Mission in a Strange New World* (Paternoster, 2004), pp. 11–12.

28. Philip Jenkins, *The Next Christendom: The Coming of Global Christianity* (OUP, 2002).

29. Cited in Jacinta Ashworth and Ian Farthing, 'Churchgoing in the UK' (Tearfund, 2007), p. 7.

30. Cited in Matthew Hughes (ed.), *Social Trends* 40 (The Office for National Statistics/Palgrave Macmillan, 2010), pp. 197–198.

31. Nick Spencer and Graham Tomlin, *The Responsive Church: Listening to Our World, Listening to God* (IVP, 2005), pp. 27–31.

32. *Mission-Shaped Church: Church Planting and Fresh Expressions of Church in a Changing Context* (Church House Publishing, 2004), p. 11.

33. Stuart Murray, 'Christendom and Post-Christendom', missionalchurchnetwork.com (www.missionalchurchnetwork.com/wp-content/uploads/2010/04/christendom-murray.pdf), p. 17.

34. The Church of England, 'Provisional Attendance Figures for 2008 Released', cofe.anglican.org, 22 January 2010 (www.cofe.anglican.org/news/pr1310.html).

35. *Mission-Shaped Church: Church Planting and Fresh Expressions of Church in a Changing Context* (Church House Publishing, 2004), p. 11.

36. John Finney, *Finding Faith Today: How Does It Happen?* (British and Foreign Bible Society, 1992), p. 57.

37. Stuart Murray, *Post-Christendom: Church and Mission in a Strange New World* (Paternoster, 2004), p. 234.

38. See Tim Chester, *Good News to the Poor* (IVP, 2004).

39. John Finney, *Finding Faith Today: How Does It Happen?* (British and Foreign Bible Society, 1992).

40. Hazel Southam, 'Church Predicts Death of Sunday School', *The Independent*, 30 July 2000 (www.independent.co.uk/news/uk/ this-britain/church-predicts-death-of-sunday-school-707079.html).

41. *Mission-Shaped Church: Church Planting and Fresh Expressions of Church in a Changing Context* (Church House Publishing, 2004), p. 40.

42. Jim Petersen, *Church Without Walls: Moving Beyond Traditional Boundaries* (NavPress, 1992), p. 111.

43. Stuart Murray, 'Christendom and Post-Christendom', missionalchurchnetwork.com (www.missionalchurchnetwork.com/ wp-content/uploads/2010/04/christendom-murray.pdf), p. 5.

44. Miroslav Volf, 'Soft Difference: Theological Reflections on the Relation Between Church and Culture in 1 Peter', *Ex Auditu* 10 (1994) (www.yale.edu/faith/downloads/soft-difference-church-culture.pdf).

45. Karen H. Jobes, *1 Peter*, Baker Exegetical Commentary on the New Testament (Baker, 2005).

46. Ibid., p. 38.

47. Ibid., p. 62.

48. Miroslav Volf, 'Soft Difference: Theological Reflections on the Relation Between Church and Culture in 1 Peter', *Ex Auditu* 10 (1994) www.yale.edu/faith/downloads/soft-difference-church-culture.pdf).

49. J. Ramsey Michaels, *1 Peter*, Word Biblical Commentary (Word, 1988), pp. xlvi–xlix.

50. Karen H. Jobes, *1 Peter*, Baker Exegetical Commentary on the New Testament (Baker, 2005), p. 1.

51. I. Howard Marshall, *1 Peter*, IVP New Testament Commentary Series (IVP Academic, 1991), p. 14.

52. P. J. Achtemeier, *1 Peter*, Hermeneia Commentary Series (Fortress, 1996), p. 174.

2. Everyday community

1. See Randy Newman, *Questioning Evangelism: Engaging People's Hearts the Way Jesus Did* (Kregel, 2004), p. 55.

2. Stuart Murray, *Post-Christendom: Church and Mission in a Strange New World* (Paternoster, 2004), p. 1.

3. Callum Brown, *The Death of Christian Britain* (Routledge, 2000), pp. 193, 198.

4. Timothy Keller, 'Late Modern or Post-modern?', redeemercitytocity. com, 4 October 2010 (redeemercitytocity.com/blog/view.jsp?Blog_param=214).

5. See www.chronologicalbiblestorying.com.

6. See www.echothestory.com.

7. Miroslav Volf, 'Soft Difference: Theological Reflections on the Relation Between Church and Culture in 1 Peter' *Ex Auditu* 10 (1994) (www.yale.edu/faith/downloads/soft-difference-church-culture.pdf).

8. From Tim Keller, 'The Missional Church', June 2001 (www.redeemer2.com/resources/papers/missional.pdf).

9. The Crowded House Values (www.thecrowedhouse.org, July 2008).

10. Karen H. Jobes, *1 Peter*, Baker Exegetical Commentary on the New Testament (Baker, 2005), p. 4.

11. Alan J. Roxburgh and M. Scott Boren, *Introducing the Missional Church* (Baker, 2009), p. 79.

12. Lois Barrett, 'Missional Witness: The Church as the Apostle to the World', in Darrell L. Guder (ed.), *Missional Church: A Vision for the Sending of the Church in Northern America* (Eerdmans, 1998), p. 127.

13. Os Guinness, *Prophetic Untimeliness: A Challenge to the Idol of Relevance* (Baker, 2003), p. 15.

14. H. Richard Niebuhr, *Christ and Culture* (Harper & Row, 1951).

15. John Howard Yoder, 'How H. Richard Niebuhr Reasoned: A Critique of *Christ and Culture*', in Glen H. Stassen, D. M. Yeager and John Howard Yoder (eds.), *Authentic Transformation: A New Vision of Christ and Culture* (Abingdon Press, 1996), p. 69.

16. Os Guinness and David Wells, 'Global Gospel, Global Era: Christian Discipleship and Mission in the Age of Globalization', The Lausanne Global Conversation, 2010 (conversation.lausanne.org/en/conversations/detail/10566/).

17. Miroslav Volf, 'Soft Difference: Theological Reflections on the Relation Between Church and Culture in 1 Peter', *Ex Auditu* 10 (1994) (www.yale.edu/faith/downloads/soft-difference-church-culture.pdf).

18. Karen H. Jobes, *1 Peter*, Baker Exegetical Commentary on the New Testament (Baker, 2005), p. 62.

19. Tim Keller, 'What Is God's Global Urban Mission?', The Lausanne Global Conversation, 2010 (conversation.lausanne.org/en/conversations/details/10282).

20. See Tim Chester and Steve Timmis, *Total Church* (IVP/Crossway, 2007/2008), ch. 3.

3. Everyday pastoral care

1. Dietrich Bonhoeffer, *Life Together* and *Psalms: Prayerbook of the Bible* (Fortress, 2005), p. 36.

2. Ibid., pp. 37–38.

3. Ibid., p. 34.

4. From Tim Chester, *You Can Change* (IVP, 2008).

4. Everyday mission

1. Nick Spencer and Graham Tomlin, *The Responsive Church: Listening to Our World, Listening to God* (IVP, 2005), p. 113.

2. Thomas R. Schreiner, *1, 2 Peter, Jude*, The New American Commentary (Broadman, 2003), p. 139.

3. John Finney, *Finding Faith Today: How Does it Happen?* (British and Foreign Bible Society, 1992).

4. Mark Greene, *The Great Divide* (The London Institute for Contemporary Christianity, 2010), p. 8.

5. Adapted from Michael Foster, 'Missions and Community Through

the Ordinary' (michaelfoster.typepad.com/blog/2008/09/ missions-and-co.html, 11 September 2008).

6. Jonathan Dobson, 'Eight Ways to Easily Be Missional', 7 April 2009 (churchplantingnovice.wordpress.com/2009/04/07/8-ways-to-easily-be-missional).

7. G. K. Beale, *The Temple and the Church's Mission: A Biblical Theology of the Dwelling Place of God* (Apollos/ IVP Academic, 2004), p. 25.

8. Paul Barnett, *Apocalypse Now and Then* (Aquila Press, 1989), p. 152.

9. Stuart Murray, *Post-Christendom: Church and Mission in a Strange New World* (Paternoster, 2004), p. 217.

10. George R. Hunsberger, 'Mission Vocation: Called and Sent to Represent the Reign of God', in Darrell L. Guder (ed.), *Missional Church: A Vision for the Sending of the Church in Northern America* (Eerdmans, 1998), p. 108.

11. Karen H. Jobes, *1 Peter*, Baker Exegetical Commentary on the New Testament (Baker, 2005), p. 204.

12. George R. Hunsberger, 'Mission Vocation: Called and Sent to Represent the Reign of God', in Darrell L. Guder (ed.), *Missional Church: A Vision for the Sending of the Church in Northern America* (Eerdmans, 1998), pp. 108–109.

13. Nick Spencer and Graham Tomlin, *The Responsive Church: Listening to Our World, Listening to God* (IVP, 2005), p. 99.

14. From Alan Hirsch with Darryn Altclass, *The Forgotten Ways Handbook* (Brazos Press, 2009), p. 97.

15. Rodney Stark, *The Rise of Christianity: How the Obscure, Marginal Jesus Movement Became the Dominant Religious Force in the Western World in a Few Centuries* (Princeton/HarperCollins, 1996/1997).

16. Cited in Leonard Verduin and Franklin Hamlin Littell, *The Reformers and Their Stepchildren* (Eerdmans, 2000), p. 28.

17. Ibid.

18. Alan Hirsch, *The Forgotten Ways: Reactivating the Missional Church* (Brazos Press, 2007), p. 85.

19. Henry Chadwick, *The Early Church* (Penguin, 1976), p. 56.

20. Michael Aquilina, 'A Double Take on Early Christianity: An Interview With Rodney Stark', 22 July 2004 (www.jknirp.com/stark.htm).

5. Everyday evangelism

1. Timothy Keller, *The Reason for God: Belief in an Age of Skepticism* (Dutton, 2008), p. 173.
2. See Nick Pollard, *Evangelism Made Slightly Less Difficult*, 'Part One: Helping People Who Don't Seem Interested' (IVP, 1997).
3. See Randy Newman, *Questioning Evangelism: Engaging People's Hearts the Way Jesus Did* (Kregel, 2004) and Tim Downs, *Finding Common Ground* (Moody, 1999), pp. 128–133.
4. On surface idols and deep idols see Julian Hardyman, *Idols: God's Battle for Our Hearts* (IVP, 2010).

6. Hope at the margins

1. Cited in Karen H. Jobes, *1 Peter*, Baker Exegetical Commentary on the New Testament (Baker, 2005), p. 89.
2. Cited in Edmund Clowney, *The Message of 1 Peter*, The Bible Speaks Today (IVP, 1999), p. 145.
3. See Tim Chester, *The Ordinary Hero: Living the Cross and Resurrection* (IVP, 2010), pp. 54–55, 122–125.
4. John Calvin, *Institutes of the Christian Religion*, trans. F. L. Battles, ed. J. T. McNeill (Westminster/SCM, 1961), vol. 1, 3.19.9.
5. See further Tim Chester, *The Busy Christian's Guide to Busyness*, 2nd edn (IVP, 2008).
6. Edmund Clowney, *The Message of 1 Peter*, The Bible Speaks Today (IVP, 1999), p. 205.

Porterbrook
TRAINING

training you to serve Jesus, his people and his world

- for church planters, leaders, and all Christians who want to become more mission-focused
- no prior theological education required
- whole-of-life training with studies in Bible, doctrine, character, church and mission
- weekly seminars or distance learning with residentials
- 5 hours of study per week with a flexible schedule

Affordable, high-quality training for mission and ministry in the 21st century. I warmly recommend it.
Tim Keller, Senior Pastor, Redeemer Presbyterian Church, NY

Porterbrook
NORTHERN TRAINING INSTITUTE

training you for leadership in the context of your ministry

- Bible college-level programme of study
- integrate theological training with involvement in ministry
- affordable
- 10-15 hours of study per week, with residential weeks, seminar days and guided reading

Directors: Tim Chester and Steve Timmis
www.theporterbrooknetwork.org